Table of Contents

1. Introduction	2
2. A Flawed System	3
3. The Structure of The Criminal Justice System	6
4. An Overview of the Criminal Justice System	13
5. The Shifting Focus of the Criminal Justice System	16
6. Looking for a Lawyer	20
7. Investigation or Pre-Charge	25
8. Pre-Trial	34
9. Analyzing Criminal Cases	48
10. The Jury Trial Process	54
11. Defending Criminal Charges at a Jury Trial	61
12. Direct Appeal	76
13. Fighting a Case After Direct Appeal	97
14. Additional Appellate Resources	115
15. Faith	118

1. Introduction

I am a criminal defense trial lawyer with over twenty-five years of experience, more than fifty felony trials and dozens of appeals. Some people believe that me and those like me stop the system from working the way it should, but those people are wrong. I am in the United States Constitution, I am in the Sixth Amendment if you are looking for me, and I defend people against "the awesome power of government". Before the government can take away the freedom or even the lives of its citizens, the government has to get past someone like me.

I am a zealous advocate, a warrior and I fight for my clients with every fiber of my being. Often, times the facts are against me, the law is against me, the public is against me, the police, the prosecution, and sometimes even the judge. Despite the odds, I still fight to find a way to win for my clients and their families.

I understand the criminal justice system in a way that few people ever will, and I wrote this book, not for the general public, not for my fellow lawyers or for law students, but for the defendants and their families that are trying to understand the criminal justice system so that they can survive it. After all my years of experience, I can tell you that the criminal justice system does not work the way that "they" tell you it does. This book explains the criminal justice system from a criminal defense lawyer's point of view. Further information about the criminal justice system can be found on my website at www.OklahomaCriminalLaw.com.

The law changes continually, so you should not assume that any case law or statute referenced in this book is still good law. **Nothing in this book should be considered legal advice. If you have a legal question, you should consult with a lawyer experienced in criminal law to discuss the specific facts of your case and advise you of your legal options.**

2. A Flawed System

Yes, the criminal justice system is flawed, it is flawed for the same reason that we need a criminal justice system to begin with; because we as people are flawed. To have a perfect system we would have to correct the flawed nature of man and then we would not need a criminal justice system. Spending time focusing on the flaws of those involved within the system or focusing on the perceived flaws of the system itself, will not help you fight your criminal case or conviction.

Those who focus their efforts on learning how the system is designed to operate and then use that understanding to either assist their lawyer in fighting their case or to fight their conviction on their own[1], have a better chance of success than those that do not understand how the system operates or that spend their time attacking those within the system. As a lawyer I have had to learn not to attack those within the system who I believed were not doing their job. This does not mean that I never point it out when "they" are not upholding the standards of the system, it means I only point that out when it advances my client's interest to do so, and I try not to personally attack those within the system. A defendant and their family should be careful not to attack the people within the system or "fight the system" for the sake of fighting the system, they generally should learn how the system is designed to work and use that knowledge of the system to fight the their criminal case or conviction.

For good or bad the criminal justice system is a representation of "the powers that be" in a particular community; for that reason, if the people involved within a particular system were removed, most often they would be replaced by others that think and act similarly. Over the years I have come to understand that the no matter how hard I have tried, I have been unable to make significant change to the system. In order to make long term lasting changes you have to change the hearts and the minds of the people in that community, because the people in that community are the ones electing the "powers that be" that shape that criminal justice system.

---

[1] I do not recommend defendants to choose to represent themselves, but I understand that after a losing direct appeal, because of a lack of money, that many defendants have no other choice.

The true "change" that I have been able to make comes in the lives of my clients and their families after I have been able to help them achieve a favorable outcome in their criminal case. If you or your loved one is currently fighting a case or conviction in the criminal justice system, remember your goal is not to change the system or to attack those within the system, your goal is to achieve a favorable outcome so that you can change your life or the life of your family member.

Problems arise in our criminal justice system when the people within the system ignore the principal of "equal justice under law" and become a "respecter of persons", meaning people are treated differently depending on who they are. When people within the system treat defendants differently based upon "who" they are, they betray the principal of "equal justice under law" and weaken our system. Most often this occurs because of the tendency of human nature to see the world with an "us verses them" or "good guy verses bad guy" mentality. When you call someone a "bad guy", that is a comparison, what you are actually saying is "I am good" and "they are bad"; if you are "good" and the other person is "bad" then whatever you have to do to stop that person becomes justifiable in your mind.

This "us verses them" mentality is a slippery slope that leads the people within the system to stop following the law themselves, why should they follow the law if in their minds they are the "good guys"[2]? The further the people within the system continue down the "good guy verses bad guy" road, the more that system becomes a system of "men" and not a system "of laws"[3]. The tendency of human nature to view the world through the "good guy verses bad guy" mentality is so strong that often times it leads to absurd justifications and eventually leads to great human cruelty, this is one of the reasons that human nature tends towards tyranny. For our system to work the way it is designed to work, those who have been

---

[2] When people within the criminal justice system refuse to follow the law themselves they are subverting the "rule of law" and replacing it with their own sense of right and wrong

[3] John Adams, founding father and second president of the united States famously said we are a "nation of laws, not of men".

entrusted with enforcing the law must actually follow the law themselves.

Often times whether a defendant is being treated fairly or unfairly within a criminal justice system will depend on whether or not the people within the system view them as a "good guy" or a "bad guy" and whether the people inside the system believe the "victim" is a "good guy" or a "bad guy".

There is a lot of irony in the criminal justice system associated with the "us verse them" mentality. It is ironic that some of the people, whose job it is to enforce the law, do not follow the law themselves and it is also ironic that some of the defendants and their families can be so angry about the people within the system not following the law, when the reason most of the defendants are going through the system is because they themselves did not follow the law either.

The best thing that defendants and their families can do is be aware of this "us verse them" mentality and not fall into the trap of thinking that way. Defense lawyers, defendants and families of the defendants have a much better chances of achieving a favorable outcome by focusing on using the system to win their criminal case, than they do by attacking those within the system who see the world through a "good guy verses bad guy mentality." It is human nature that when people are attacked, they are more likely to revert into the "us verses them mentality" which is generally not in a defendant's best interest. The best strategy for a defendant who believes they are being treated unfairly is for their lawyer to make a record about how the law is not being followed so that they can appeal the erroneous decisions to a higher court. The defense must always keep in mind that no one needs the rule of law more than the accused, it is the rule of law that protects defendants from tyranny of the majority.

3. The Structure of the Criminal Justice System

Our criminal justice system is designed using the the principal of separation of powers and understanding that principal will help you to understand how our system works.

A democratic society, in which respect for the dignity of all men is central, naturally guards against the misuse of the law enforcement process....**The awful instruments of the criminal law cannot be entrusted to a single functionary. The complicated process of criminal justice is therefore divided into different parts, responsibility for which is separately vested in the various participants upon whom the criminal law relies for its vindication.**

McNabb v. United States, 318 U.S. 332, 343 (1943).

The brilliance of the United States Constitution is the separation of powers. America's founding fathers understood human nature tended towards tyranny and that the separation of powers is our best protection against the abuse of power. In the American justice system power is separated between and within each branch of government. To accomplish the purpose of a government, at a minimum you must have three things. Someone has to make the laws (The Legislative Branch-Article I of the United States Constitution), someone has to enforce the laws (The Executive Branch-Article II of the United States Constitution) and someone has to interpret the laws (The Judicial Branch-Article III of the United States Constitution).

In both the state and federal criminal justice systems the legislative branch of government passes bills defining what behavior is criminal, the punishment for each crime and the criminal procedure that will be used to make legal determinations. If the chief executive (president or the governor) agrees with the bill passed by the legislature, they will sign the bill into law, and if they do not agree they will veto the bill. The courts also play a role in the making of laws, the courts interpret the laws passed by the legislature and if a law is challenged as unconstitutional the courts determine whether or not the challenged law passes constitutional muster.

Criminal laws are often times a product of all three branches of government over a period of years. For example a law may have been passed decades ago, but the circumstances that the law applies to has been interpreted (or refined) by court decisions over the years. As a result the legal decisions that a trial judge makes on a defendant's case may be influenced by years of legal opinions (also called *stare decisis*[4] or case law). It is not unusual for judges to personally disagree with the legal conclusions that they feel compelled to reach in a particular cases. Over the years I have had judges tell me "off the record" that they did not like the conclusion that they reached, but they believed that the law required that they reach that conclusion. So if the judge reaches a legal conclusion that you wish they had not reached in your case, keep in mind the judge may have wished they could have reached a different legal conclusion as well, but felt that the proper application the law required them to reach the decision that they reached. Regardless of whether the judge wanted to reach that decision or not, keep in mind your goal is not to change the system, your goal is to get a favorable outcome on your case.

A great example of the progression of the law over the years is the right to counsel, the right to counsel is a defendant's right to have a lawyer assist him or her in their defense, even if the defendant does not have the ability to pay for the lawyer. The right is rooted in the Sixth Amendment of the United States Constitution for defendants facing federal criminal charges and for defendants facing state criminal charges the right to counsel is applied to them by what is known as the "incorporation doctrine", which incorporates (or applies) to the states, parts of the first Ten Amendments to the United States Constitution (the Bill of Rights) through the Due Process clause of the Fourteenth Amendment.

The right to counsel for indigent state court defendants first started to take root in 1932 in the case of *Powell v. Alabama*, 287 U.S. 45 (1932)[5] when the United States Supreme Court reversed a death sentence given to an indigent unrepresented defendant after he was convicted of rape. Ten years later in *Betts v. Brady*, 316 U.S. 455 (1942) the Supreme Court ruled an indigent state court defendant <u>was not</u> entitled to the right to counsel for state felony charges that

---

[4] The legal principle of determining issues in cases in the same manner as previous cases.

[5] The defendants in this case were known as the "Scottsboro Boys".

did not carry the death penalty. However, twenty-one years later *Betts v. Brady* was reversed, when the United States Supreme Court finally ruled that a state court indigent defendant was entitled to legal representation for felony charges in the case of *Gideon v. Wainwright*, 372 U.S. 335 (1963).

If you go all the way back to the ratification of the Sixth Amendment, which occurred in 1791, it took 172 years for the Sixth Amendment right to counsel for indigent state court defendants charged with "non-death penalty" felonies to become a reality, and if you just go back the the Supreme Court's decision in *Powell v. Alabama* the right took over 30 years to be recognized by the Supreme Court. The point is that many different people in different branches of our government over many years played a role in the development of that area of law, so if you do not agree with the law on that point, who are you going to be angry with? And the more important question is, how is being angry over the current state of the law going to help you or your loved one get a more favorable outcome?

Shaped by the principal of separation of powers, many aspects of criminal law has developed over the years through the efforts of those within the different branches of state and federal governments. For example, before evidence can be admitted at a federal criminal trial the evidence must meet the requirements of the Federal Rules of Evidence (see FRE 101(b)(2) and 402). The Federal Rules of Evidence were originally adopted by the United States Supreme Court in 1972 and were later passed in a bill by Congress and in 1975 were signed into law by President Gerald Ford.

After the Federal Rules of Evidence were codified into law, judges began applying the rules to the cases before them, when those judge's decisions interpreting the law were appealed to higher courts, a body of "case law" was developed over the years regarding the Federal Rules of Evidence. Often times when a judge allows the introduction of evidence that is harmful to a defendant, a defendant or their family will start criticizing the judge for the ruling. More often then not the judge has made the correct legal decision, or a decision that is within the judge's discretion, and what the defendant and or their family are actually complaining about is the current state of the law or the rule of evidence itself. If you disagree with the current state of the law or a rule of evidence, there are many people over lots of years to disagree with. It is important to keep in mind that the system operates the way that it does for many reasons and just because it does not work the way that you think that it should work does not mean the system is wrong and you are right.

Many defendants and their families make the mistake of attacking the system or people within the system when the people within the system are making the legally correct decisions. Watching the reaction of the defendant's family and the victim's family to judicial rulings made within a case often times reminds me of the way that sports fans react to decisions made by referees in a sporting event, if the call goes against their side they believe the decision was wrong and if the the call goes in favor of their side they believe it was the right decision.

For a criminal defendant, the right to trial by jury[6] is among the most valuable constitutional rights they have, and is part of the protection of the Doctrine of Separation of Powers in the United States Constitution. The right to trial by jury, separates the power to determine "guilt or innocence" from those that have the power to bring the criminal charges. In the American justice system the jurors are the "finders of fact" and they decide whether or not the government has proven the defendant's guilt by proving every element, of every offense, beyond a reasonable doubt. The "right to trial by jury" protects people from "the awesome power of government", it removes the power to determine guilt or innocence from the government who brings the charges and gives that power to average citizens; considering the course of human history, the right to trial by jury is truly remarkable. This is not to say that most defendants <u>should</u> exercise their right to trial by jury, most defendants are better off asking their lawyers to negotiate the best plea agreement they can negotiate and resolving their criminal cases with a plea; but, when it is needed, the right to trial by jury protects the people from the tyranny of government officials.

Because of the separation of powers, different branches of the government have different roles within our criminal justice system.

---

[6] For federal court defendants the Right to Trial by Jury is founded in the *6th Amendment* and for state court defendants its is founded in the *Fourteenth Amendment*.

Inherent in the power to legislate is the power to define, the legislature determines what is and is not a crime, what the "elements" of each crime will be, and the range of punishment for each offense. The legislature also defines what the rules of evidence are, the criminal procedure, and the statutory rights a criminal defendant will have.

The prosecutor, who is a member of the executive branch, "enforces" the law through prosecution. Every crime has "elements" and in order to convict the accused of a crime at trial, a prosecutor must prove every element of the crime beyond a reasonable doubt. However, the prosecutor only has to prove the elements of a crime and does not have to prove things that are not elements[7].

Just as the legislature has the power to define by passing legislation, the judiciary also has the power to interpret and define the laws with their opinions. If the defense disagrees with a decision of a judge, they generally have to wait until and address, what they believe to be erroneous decisions by the judge, on appeal if the defendant is convicted.

Due Process of Law is another important principal of the American criminal justice system. The fundamental fairness of the criminal justice system is protected by the constitutional right of Due Process of law.

> Cases in this Court have long proceeded on the premise that the Due Process Clause guarantees the fundamental elements of fairness in a criminal trial.

Spencer v. Texas, 385 U.S. 554, 563-64 (1967)

However, the power of the courts to protect the fundamental fairness of the criminal justice system does not give the courts the power to substitute their judgment, for the judgment of the legislature, this is know as "judicial restraint" and is an important feature of the separation of powers. Legislators have discretion in doing their job and the courts generally respect the discretion of the legislature, as an independent and separate branch of government. Legislators are elected and if the general public does not like the laws they enact, the public can vote them out of office; federal judges and

---

[7] With most crimes the prosecution does not have to prove motive.

many of the appellate judges are appointed and cannot be simply voted out of office. Our system is designed to give the public a greater control over the governmental rule making decisions of the criminal justice system by having those decisions made by the politicians who regularly stand for election; as long as those rules do not violate the constitutional rights of the accused.

Judicial restraint, also applies to federal courts when they review state court criminal convictions. This too is a separation of powers issue, separation of powers operates not just between the different branches of the same government, but also between state and federal governments.

Federal courts regularly exercise judicial restraint when it comes to determining whether or not a state's rule of law or practice violates a defendant's constitutional rights, by doing so they are attempting to strike a balance between the the rights of the accused and the rights of the citizens of that state to govern their own affairs.

Prosecutors, law enforcement officers and other members of the executive branch have a certain amount of discretion in exercising their executive power. Courts may decide during a criminal prosecution whether or not law enforcement has violated the rights of a defendant, or whether or not there is sufficient evidence to proceed with a criminal prosecution, or other similar issues; however, the discretionary decisions made by members of the executive branch are typically not reviewable by the judiciary.

Often times defendants and their families will ask questions such as "why doesn't the judge just dismiss the case?" Frequently the reason that the judge doesn't "just dismiss the case" is because the judge cannot just "dismiss" the case unless there is a legal reason to dismiss the case. The prosecutor represents the executive branch and has the "discretion" to bring criminal charges; unless there is a legal reason for the case to be dismissed, judges are without the legal authority to dismiss a criminal case. The judge cannot override the prosecutor's discretion and "dismiss" a case just because the judge does not believe the prosecutor should exercise his or her discretion in the way the prosecutor has exercised it, this is a feature of the separation of powers of our criminal justice system[8].

While the separation of powers doctrine may frustrate some defendants and their families, the separation of powers is an important protection that is built into our criminal justice system and one of the most brilliant features of the United Sates Constitution. The separation of powers feature of our criminal justice system is much more likely to benefit a defendant, than it is to benefit a government actor who is part of the power structure.

---

[8] *Albright v. Oliver*, 510 U.S. 266, 297 n.11 (1994) ("*Wayte v. United States*, 470 U.S. 598, 607 (1985); *Bordenkircher v. Hayes*, 434 U.S. 357, 364 (1978) ("In our system, so long as the prosecutor has probable cause to believe that the accused committed an offense defined by statute, the decision whether or not to prosecute, and what charge to file or bring before a grand jury, generally rests entirely in his discretion"")

4. An Overview of the Criminal Justice System
Investigative or Pre-Charge Stage

Law enforcement investigates criminal accusations to determine if probable cause exist that a crime was committed and the defendant committed the crime. If law enforcement concludes that probable cause exist, they may either arrest the defendant or present an "out of custody affidavit" and the defendant will be arrested on a warrant if formal charges are filed by the prosecution. The results of law enforcement's investigation are given to the prosecution who makes the decision of whether or not to file formal charges.

Pre-Trial

Defendants have a right to an independent (independent from the prosecution and law enforcement) determination of probable cause when charged with a felony, sometimes this independent determination is made by a grand jury before formal charges are filed and sometimes this independent determination is made by a judge after formal charges are filed. If the grand jury makes the independent determination, that occurs before formal charges are filed and defendants and their lawyers have little to no participation in that process. If a judge makes the independent determination that occurs after formal charges are filed at a preliminary hearing, and defendants and their lawyers are allowed to participate in that process.

Once probable cause has been independently established, a defendant must generally choose between entering a plea to the charge in hopes of reducing (mitigating) their punishment or trying the case to a jury in hopes of preventing the prosecution from proving their guilt beyond a reasonable doubt.

However, after an independent determination of probable cause has been made, the defense may be able to file a dispositive motion that forces the dismissal of the case, if the defense has a sufficient factual and legal basis. These types of motions could include arguments such as a lack of jurisdiction, statute of limitations, a motion to suppress the evidence[9] the prosecution needs to establish probable cause or some other legal prohibition against prosecution.

---

[9] You can not generally suppress the testimony of the witnesses, so if there are witnesses that establish probable cause: most of the time, the defendant's guilt or innocence is a question of fact for a jury.

Each criminal justice system will have its own criminal procedure to ensure things such as defendants are represented by counsel, to establish conditions of bond or release pending trial, are given notice of the charges they are facing and the evidence the government has against them, jury selection, trial, and a process to enter pleas of guilty and or to determine the appropriate sentence.

Trial

If a defendant chooses to proceed to trial each criminal justice system will have a process for the selection of a jury, presentation of the evidence, the right to confront the witnesses against the defendant, the use of the court's process to compel presentation of favorable evidence and witnesses, the right to present witnesses, the right of the defendant to testify, instruction on the applicable law and other Due Process rights. These processes can vary widely; however, they must at a minimum meet the constitutional standards of due process.

Post-Trial

If a defendant is acquitted (found not guilty) by a jury, there can be no appeal because of Double Jeopardy. If a defendant is convicted they must be given an opportunity to appeal their conviction and challenge the legal process that produced their conviction. If a defendant is convicted in the federal system, they appeal their conviction to the appropriate federal circuit court and then on to the United States Supreme Court, if they loose their appeal at the federal circuit court. If a defendant is convicted in a state criminal justice system, they must appeal their conviction using the system established by the state they were convicted in. A state court defendant can file a Petition for a Writ of Certiorari to the United States Supreme Court and ask that Court to review the denial of their appeal by the highest criminal court in the state they were convicted in, if they have an issue that involves a federal statutory or constitutional right. A Petition for a Writ of Certiorari to the United States Supreme Court, is a request that the Court review the case, these request are rarely granted.

If after exhausting their state court remedies, a defendant convicted in state court believes that their federal rights were violated and state appellate court reached a conclusion that was contrary to clearly established federal law or was an "unreasonable determination of the facts in light of the evidence presented in the state court proceeding", they can appeal that decision into their local federal district court using the federal habeas statute. If a state court defendant is denied their habeas petition at the federal district court level, they can appeal that denial to the appropriate federal circuit court. If a federal habeas appeal is denied at the circuit court level, a defendant can ask the United States Supreme Court to review that denial by filing a Petition for a Writ of Certiorari with the United States Supreme Court.

After appealing to the highest court in the criminal justice system they were convicted in, appealing to the United States Supreme Court, appealing all the way through the federal habeas system, and back to the United States Supreme Court, state court criminal convictions are typically[10] final unless the defendant is able to secure a commutation or a pardon which is a remedy from the executive branch, not the judicial branch.

---

[10] There is a concept in the law known as "actual innocence" that could conceivably serve as a "gateway" to bypass procedural defaults and or statute of limitations if a defendant were able to show that a constitutional violation has likely resulted in the conviction of one that is actually innocent. See *Schule v. Delo*, 513 U.S. 298 (1995) and also *Herra v. Collins*, 506 U.S. 390 (1993). However, you must also read the case of *Shinn v. Ramirez*, 142 S. Ct. 1718 (2022) which is not favorable to defendants.

5. The Shifting Focus of the Criminal Justice System

The proper focus in defending a criminal case changes as a case makes its way through the criminal justice system, this is because as a case proceeds through the criminal justice system the legal test and burdens change, and as a result the proper focus changes.

The beginning of the criminal justice system is the investigative or pre-charges phase. The goal of the officer conducting the investigation is to collect enough evidence to establish "probable cause[11]", which is enough evidence to make a reasonable person believe that a crime was probably committed and that the defendant probably committed the crime. The investigation could begin with "reasonable suspicion[12]" or "probable cause[13]" during a traffic stop, it could begin with an officer witnessing suspicious behavior or the commission of a crime, it could begin with a 911 call, the service of a search warrant or someone showing up to the police department to file a police report. Regardless of how the investigation begins, probable cause is the investigating officer's goal. In the investigative officer's pursuit of evidence many different legal issues that may arise, but all of the legal issues typically revolve around the lawfulness of the collection of the evidence that the prosecution will use to establish probable cause and to prosecute the defendant.

The law enforcement officer investigating the case, the prosecutor making the charging decision on the case, and the judge who signs either a search warrant and or and arrest warrant are all primarily focused on whether or not probable cause exist. Since the system is focused on probable cause, competent defense counsel should also be focused on probable cause. Why is everyone so focused on probable cause during the investigatory phase of a criminal case? Because probable cause is the applicable legal

---

[11] *Brinegar v. United States*, 338 U.S. 160, 175 (1949) ("In dealing with probable cause, however, as the very name implies, we deal with probabilities. These are not technical; they are the factual and practical considerations of everyday life on which reasonable and prudent men, not legal technicians, act. The standard of proof is accordingly correlative to what must be proved. "The substance of all the definitions" of probable cause "is a reasonable ground for belief of guilt."")

[12] *Terry v. Ohio*, 392 U.S. 1 (1968); see also *US v. Coleman*, 969 F.2d 126 (5th Cir. 1992)

[13] *US v. Degasso*, 369 F.3d 1139 (10th Circuit 2004)

standard and without probable cause search warrants are not issued, charges are not filed, and or the case is dismissed without trial. That is not to say that the investigator, the prosecutor, and the defense attorney will not also be concerned with other issues such as whether or not there is enough evidence to prove the accusations to a jury beyond a reasonable doubt, but probable cause is the primary focus during the investigative phase.

Before charges are filed, during the investigation of an accusation the proper focus for a criminal defendant and a criminal defense attorney should generally be on:

1. not giving law enforcement anything that could be used to establish probable cause that the defendant committed a crime

2. and on the gathering of evidence that the defense may need if charges are filed

Occasionally, the facts and circumstances will be right for an experienced criminal lawyer to take proactive steps to prevent the filing of criminal charges, but in most cases the best course of action is for a defendant to exercise their right to remain silent and wait to see if the government has enough evidence to file charges, while gathering and preserving evidence that they will need in the event that charges are filed.

After charges are filed, during the pre-trial phase, the defense should focus on evaluating the charges to determine if there are any dispositive motions that could get the case dismissed prior to trial, such as a motion to suppress. If the evidence the government is using to establish probable cause, was obtained in violation of the defendant's constitutional rights, a lawyer can file a motion to suppress. If the motion to suppress is granted, it will deprive the government of the evidence the government needs to establish probable cause and as a result the case will be dismissed without having to go to trial. If a lawyer files a motion to suppress on a case they have no intention of trying to a jury, and even if the motion to suppress is granted there will still be probable cause for the case to proceed, the lawyer is probably doing so because they are focused on something they should not be focused upon; something like justifying the fee they have been paid or fighting for the sake of fighting. Focusing on the wrong things generally leads to poor results.

During this stage of the case a decision is generally made on whether or not to proceed to trial, or to resolve the case with a plea (ultimately this is the client's decision). If the case is going to be resolved with a plea, the focus shifts to the mitigation of punishment. If the case is not going to be resolved with a plea, the focus becomes trial preparation.

Once the defense begins preparing for a jury[14] trial, the primary focus of the defense becomes preventing the government from proving guilt beyond a reasonable doubt and or mitigating punishment if convicted. Sometimes the defense decides to try a case to a jury seeking a complete acquittal of all charges, sometimes the defense is trying a case to a jury in hopes of being acquitted of the greater offense and convicted of a lesser offense and sometimes, depending on whether the jury recommends[15] punishment or not, the defense is trying a case to the jury for punishment. If the defense does not know why they are trying the case to a jury, there should be a reevaluation of the strategy in the case.

Post-trial, after conviction while on appeal, the focus of the defense is on getting the conviction reversed by proving the unfairness of the process used to convict the defendant. After conviction the focus is on process and is no longer on the guilt or innocence[16] of the defendant. Appeals are about the process that was used to convict the defendant and are not an opportunity to argue that the appellate court should substitute their own judgment for the jury's judgement.[17] At a jury trial, factual determinations regarding guilt

---

[14] Technically if both sides agree the case could be tried to a judge and not a jury, with rare exceptions, this is a very bad idea.

[15] This depends on the system the case is being tried within. In Oklahoma the jury recommends punishment and in federal court they do not recommend punishment.

[16] This is the most difficult thing for convicted defendants and their families to understand and or accept after conviction.

[17] This is a separation of powers issue, I can assure you defendants and their families do not want judges to make factual determinations of guilt and innocence. In some countries appellate court's can reverse the acquittal of a defendant at the trial court, thankfully America is not one of them.

and innocence are made by the "finder of fact", which is the jury and the jury's determination of facts are not open for debate on appeal, unless as a matter of law there was insufficient evidence for the jury to have reached their verdict. An appeal is a process complaint, not a complaint that the jury should have reached a different conclusion. Appeals are about process, the fairness of the process that was used to convict the defendant and the appellate process that is in place to challenge the conviction. On appeal if you are not using proper appellate process to persuade the appellate court that the criminal process used to convict the defendant at trial was seriously flawed, you are almost certainly losing.

6. Looking for a Lawyer
Do You Really Need a Lawyer?

Just because someone has made an accusation against you or is threatening to file a police report against you does not mean you need a lawyer. While there is nothing wrong with talking with a lawyer, there is not much a lawyer can do during the investigation of a criminal accusation other than to tell you to remain silent and not give a statement to law enforcement. Just keep in mind when you start talking with lawyers, that some lawyers are better businessmen than they are lawyers, and some lawyers use their persuasive abilities to make money instead of doing what is in their client's best interest. However, if you or a loved one has been arrested it is probably time to hire a lawyer.

What Type of a Criminal Lawyer do You Need?

To know what type of criminal lawyer you need, you need to figure out what you are hoping that lawyer can do for you on your case. Are you looking to work out the best plea agreement you can work out and move on with your life? Then hire a "tour guide". Most criminal lawyers are what I would refer to as "tour guides"[18], they are going to guide you through the criminal justice system and explain things to you, but they are not going to do a whole lot of advocating. There is nothing wrong with a lawyer being a tour guide, as long as they don't trick their client into thinking they are something else. Tour guides have lots of clients, payment plans and are looking to work out a plea agreement and plead their clients guilty. If you are not charged with anything too serious, you are guilty, know you are guilty and want to plead guilty, save yourself some money and hire a "tour guide". A "tour guide" is what most criminal defendants need.

Sometimes people accused of crimes know they do not want to try the case to a jury, but they believe they may have a legal issue that could possibly result in their case being dismissed. If you fall in this category you don't want a "tour guide" as I would call them, you want a lawyer that is more of an advocate. You want a lawyer that "puts on preliminary hearings" from time to time, that writes serious motions that cite to transcripts and argue case law, a lawyer that may

---

[18] Just because I would refer to most criminal lawyers as tour guides, does not mean they would refer to themselves that way.

not be a "trial lawyer", but they have had the occasional trial. Perhaps this lawyer also handles cases in federal court or does the occasional appeal. This lawyer is going to be more experienced, have fewer clients, general charge you more and be less flexible with a payment plans.

If you are charged with or suspected of a serious crime, you need a serious lawyer, a trial lawyer. Even if you are not planning on proceeding to trial, you should consider hiring a lawyer with significant jury trial experience. Most of the time there are many opportunities to resolve a criminal case long before it reaches a jury trial. However, there is no guarantee that the prosecutor will see the case from your prospective or offer a resolution that you can live with. If the prosecutor assigned to your case does not offer a resolution that you are willing to accept, without a trial lawyer representing you, proceeding to jury trial may not be a viable option. If there is a good chance you will proceed to a jury trial, you need an experienced criminal defense trial attorney. Jury trials are war and if you are going to war you better find yourself a warrior.

Here are some questions that will help you determine if the lawyer you are considering hiring is a serious lawyer, a trial lawyer.
- Has the lawyer had at least 10[19] jury trials as lead counsel?
- Has the lawyer won any of those trials? If so how many? Will the lawyer give you a list of jury trials they have had so you can verify what they are telling you?
- Does the lawyer go to Federal Court? Whether a criminal lawyer goes to Federal Court is a big dividing line among lawyers.
- Does the lawyer handle criminal appeals?
- Is the lawyer peer rated on Martindale.com?
- Has the lawyer ever handled or worked on any death penalty cases?
- Does the lawyer write serious motions or just file "canned" form motions? Ask to see some of the lawyers writings. Is the motion over 2 to 3 pages? Is the lawyer actually arguing the

---

[19] Personally I would want many more jury trials than 10, but 10 is the minimum unless you have no other choice. There is also a big difference in trying a case as a defense lawyer then as a prosecutor.

law and applying the law to the facts? Or is the lawyer just asking the judge to do something without any legal analysis?

How to Talk to Potential Lawyers

If you are able to hire a lawyer, the way that you approach potential lawyers is important. If you approach potential lawyers wrong, it can make it difficult to find a lawyer or it can influence the price you may have to pay. Lawyers reject potential clients because they come across as being "difficult" or "high maintenance" and lawyers also charge "difficult" or "high maintenance" clients more. This is very important in leaving messages for lawyers. I have had many people, after I have turned down their case ask questions like "why can't I find a lawyer" or say something like "why won't anyone call me back".

Do not start calling around trying to "sell your case", by persuading potential lawyers things such as your "rights were violated", the police "illegally searched" you, or that you know that "the case will be easy to win". People that try to "sell" their case to lawyers will generally either have a difficult time finding a lawyer (because they come across as unreasonable) or they run into a lawyer that tells them what they want to hear and takes their money with no real prospect of accomplishing what they are hoping for.

Simply tell potential lawyers about your case, do not try and sell it to them. Keep in mind you are calling a lawyer that has a doctorate degree in law and often times years of experience and making statements like "the police violated my rights"[20] will often times send up red flags about whether or not they should accept you as a client. Most criminal lawyers clearly understand that some officers do violate the rights of their clients, they also understand that it is typically not that black and white and it is difficult to get a court to rule in their client's favor. If you think law enforcement violated your rights, by all means tell your lawyer or any potential lawyer, but I would not be so adamant about it.

---

[20] If you believe that your rights were violated by all means tell the lawyer, but I recommend you not be so insistent about it. "I think the police may have violated my rights" or "I suspect" or " I wander", sends an entirely different signal to the lawyer than someone that makes a statement as if it is an indisputable fact.

A lawyer considering taking a case wants to know certain things about the case so they can evaluate whether not this is a case they are willing to accept. Lawyers want to know things like:
1. if you or the person you are calling about has been arrested or accused of a crime
2. what is the crime they have been arrested for or accused of
3. have they been arrested or is there an outstanding warrant
4. which court are the charges filed in
5. what is the case number
6. when is the next court date
7. have there been other lawyers on the case
8. what stage of the criminal process the case is in
9. what you are hoping the lawyer can accomplish
10. has the person bonded out of jail or how much is their bond
11. are you or the person you are calling about currently on probation
12. have you or the person you are calling about ever been in trouble before and if so for what

When a lawyer knows the basic information about the case they can put your story in context and identify the important information as they hear it, so do not launch in to some story trying to convince the lawyer of something. If you are contacting a lawyer for potential representation you may want to say something like "I am looking for a lawyer to represent me on a felony domestic assault and battery charge in _____ county, I am hoping the lawyer can get the case dismissed because my wife is not going to cooperate with the prosecution." People who are straight and to the point typically have a much easier time finding legal representation and they are more likely to be quoted lower fees.

You are looking for a lawyer that is a good fit for your case, not a lawyer that tells you what you want to hear before taking your money. You want to make sure that the lawyer you hire believes that he or she can get the outcome that you are hoping for. This is the problem with the people who are trying to "sell" their case to lawyers. Instead of asking the lawyer if the lawyer believes the outcome they are hoping for is realistic, they are trying to convince the lawyer the outcome they are hoping for is realistic and often times it seems like the person they are actually trying to convince is themselves.

Some common goals, that people want, when charged with a crime are;
1. Working out the best deal possible
2. Staying out of jail or prison
3. Keeping the charge "off" their record
4. Getting the case dismissed
5. Try the case to a jury

It is also important to understand that lawyers are trained to think about criminal cases in the context of the legal system and not from a personal context, as a result things that my seem important to a person facing charges will not necessarily be important to a lawyer, because the system itself may consider those things to be irrelevant. So just because a lawyer does not think or agree that certain things about the case are important, does not mean that the lawyer is uncaring, insensitive, a jerk or not giving you good advice. As an expert in the law, you should expect a lawyer to focus on things that the law considers important, because those are the things that are most likely to lead to a positive outcome in your case. What the law considers to be important is often times different than what a defendant and his or her family will think is important.

Written Fee Agreements

If your lawyer does not offer a written fee agreement, you should ask for a written fee agreement. Make sure the fee agreement addresses issues such as whether or not the fee is a hourly rate or a flat fee and if a flat fee what services are covered by the flat fee. (Most criminal lawyers accept criminal cases on flat fee agreements.) I would not recommend hiring any lawyer that was not willing to give you a written fee agreement.

7. Investigation or Pre-Charge

Investigation

When a law enforcement officer investigates a criminal accusation, what is the law enforcement officer looking for? Probable cause. Probably cause is enough evidence to establish that a crime was probably committed and enough evidence to establish the suspect probably committed the crime[21]. Probable cause is what drives the criminal justice system from the time an accusation is made until trial preparation begins. Once the officer has probable cause that a crime is committed and that the target of the investigation probably committed a crime, the officer has enough evidence to arrest the suspect and or forward the reports from their investigation to the prosecution, so the prosecution can make a charging decision. This is not to say, that the law enforcement officers will will stop the investigation once they believe they have probable cause, most officers will continue their investigation after they have enough evidence to establish probable cause, so they can make the case is as strong as possible.

Probable cause plays an important role in the criminal justice system. To search a vehicle without a warrant, an officer needs to have probable cause[22]. To have a search warrant issued by a judge, the search warrant affidavit must provide facts that are sufficient to establish probable cause[23]. For an officer to make a felony arrest without a warrant (outside of the suspect's home) all that officer must

---

[21] "Probable Cause" as it relates to charging a defendant with a crime has been defined by the Supreme Court as "facts and circumstances sufficient to warrant a prudent man in believing that the (suspect) had committed or was committing an offense." See *Beck v. Ohio*, 379 U.S. 89, 91, 85 S.Ct. 223, 225, 13 L.Ed.2d 142 (1964). Other courts have defined probable cause slightly differently, but always similarly.

[22] A police officer has probable cause to conduct a search when "the facts available to [him] would 'warrant a [person] of reasonable caution in the belief' " that contraband or evidence of a crime is present. *Florida v. Harris*, 568 U.S. 237, 243 (2013))

[23] "...valid warrants may be issued to search *any* property, whether or not occupied by a third party, at which there is probable cause to believe that fruits, instrumentalities, or evidence of a crime will be found." *Zurcher v. Stanford Daily*, 436 U.S. 547, 554 (1978)

have is probable cause[24]. For a prosecutor to file an "Information" or a "Complaint" against a defendant, the prosecutor needs probable cause. For a grand jury to return an "Indictment" the grand jurors must be persuaded that the government has established probable cause[25]. For a judge to issue an arrest warrant for a defendant, the judge must determine that the prosecution has probable cause[26]. And before a state court defendant can be "bound over for trial" on a felony charge at a "preliminary hearing" the magistrate must be persuaded that the prosecution has introduced enough evidence to establish probable cause[27].

Probable cause takes on two forms in the criminal justice system, one is probable cause of a crime and the other is probable cause to believe evidence of a crime will be found. One relates to arrest and charging of a crime and the other relates to searching for evidence of a crime.

Once the prosecution has enough evidence to establish probable cause that a crime was committed and probable cause that the defendant committed the crime, the case is going to trial unless the defendant enters a plea, there is a legal issue that forces the dismissal of the case (a dispositive motion), or the prosecution decides to dismiss the case. The existence of probable cause typically forces a defendant to choose between entering a plea in an attempt to lessen the punishment, or proceeding to trial.

Since it is the goal of a law enforcement officer to collect enough evidence to establish probable cause that a crime was committed and probable cause the defendant committed a crime, in almost all cases a defendant's best strategy is to exercise their constitutional right to

---

[24] *Carroll v. United States*, 267 U.S. 132, 156 (1925)

[25] *Gerstein v. Pugh*, 420 U.S. 103, 118 n.19 (1975) ("By contrast, the Court has held that an indictment, "fair upon its face," and returned by a "properly constituted grand jury," conclusively determines the existence of probable cause and requires issuance of an arrest warrant without further inquiry. *Ex parte United States*, 287 U.S. 241, 250 (1932).")

[26] *Manuel v. City of Joliet*, 137 S. Ct. 911, 919 n.6 (2017) (" An arrest warrant, after all, is a way of initiating legal process, in which a magistrate finds probable cause that a person committed a crime.")

[27] *State v. Juarez* , 2013 OK CR 6, ¶ 8, 299 P.3d 870, 872 ; *Kennedy v. State* , 1992 OK CR 67, ¶ 13, 839 P.2d 667, 670-71

remain silent, and do not give the investigating officer anything that could be used to establish probable cause. This does not mean that the defense tries to stop or obstruct the investigating officer from obtaining evidence to establish probable cause, because that would be an additional crime. Do not expect a defense lawyer to advise you to destroy evidence or discourage witnesses from talking with law enforcement, reputable defense attorneys do not do that and lawyers that engage in that type of behavior risk being charged with a crime themselves. Keep in mind that you need a lawyer with strong ethics, because a lawyer with weak ethics will not continue to fight for you, when fighting for you becomes difficult.

When dealing with an unrepresented person that a lawyer knows has a conflict of interest with their client (or reasonably may have a conflict of interest with their client), the only advice a lawyer can ethically give is for that person to seek the advice of counsel[28]. Regardless of whether or not a witness wants to cooperate with law enforcement, if they have (or could have) evidence that is incriminating against a lawyer's client, there is a conflict of interest with that person.

Both victims and witnesses have a right to refuse to talk with law enforcement, but generally that right not to talk to law enforcement does not extend to the right not to testify if subpoenaed as a witness to a grand jury or other court hearing, unless there is something about their testimony that may incriminate them. If the truthful testimony of a victim or a witness would have the tendency to incriminate that victim or witness in a crime, that victim or witness has a constitutional right to assert their Fifth Amendment Right against self incrimination.

If a witness to a felony refuses to attend a court proceeding to testify, or if "there is probable cause to believe that the person would be unwilling to accept service of a subpoena or may otherwise refuse to appear in any criminal proceeding...", Oklahoma law does allow law enforcement to detain a material witness, even without a warrant

---

[28] "...The lawyer shall not give legal advice to an unrepresented person, other than the advice to secure counsel, if the lawyer knows or reasonably should know that the interests of such a person are or have a reasonable possibility of being in conflict with the interests of the client." See the ABA Model Rules of Professional Conduct Rule 4.3

issued by a judge, but the law requires that they be taken in front of a judge within 48 hours. (*See* Title 22 O.S. §720) Sometimes a witness's status as a "victim" gives them the ability to refuse to cooperate, even if subpoenaed, without the fear of being arrested or having a material witness warrant issued for their arrest; this is because some states protect victims of crimes from being arrested as a material witness. Oklahoma is one of those states, "no person may be detained as a material witness to a crime who is a victim of such crime."(*See* Title 22 O.S. §720)

The federal material witness statute does not have a "victim" exception to the arrest of a material witness. However, under federal law, law enforcement is not given the right to arrest a material witness on their own, under federal law a "a judicial officer" must order the arrest of a material witness. (See 18 U.S.C. §3144) Each jurisdiction will have its own law to address this issue and a victim or a witness who has questions regarding their legal rights should consult an experienced criminal lawyer that is licensed in the jurisdiction regarding their rights.

An Important Point Regarding Due Process of Law

The difference between the way that Oklahoma law and federal law treats material witnesses is a good place to make a point about due process of law. Oklahoma law allows law enforcement in felony cases to arrest a material witness "...if there is probable cause to believe that the person would be unwilling to accept service of a subpoena or may otherwise refuse to appear in any criminal proceeding...". While federal law does not give law enforcement the authority to arrest on probable cause, but instead requires a judicial officer to order the arrest of the person if "it appears from an affidavit filed by a party that the testimony of a person is material in a criminal proceeding, and if it is shown that it may become impracticable to secure the presence of the person by subpoena".

One statute gives the discretion to arrest to law enforcement and the other gives the discretion to the judge. One statute does not allow for the arrest of a victim as a material witness and the other has no such prohibition. One statute only allows the government to seek the arrest of a material witness and the other statute allows a "party", which includes a defendant, to seek the arrest of a material witness.

Why are there such big differences between the two material witness statutes? One was passed by the Oklahoma Legislature and signed into law by the Oklahoma governor and the other was passed by Congress and signed into law by the President of the United States, in other words these are political decisions made by the politicians who were elected to make these decisions. While the word "political" is often used in a negative sense, no negative sense is meant in the way it is used here. We want citizens to influence the criminal justice system through the election of their representatives.

Since the federal statute requires the approval of a judge and the state statute allows an officer to detain a material witness if the officer believes that probable cause exist, does the state statute violate the due process rights of the witness? The answer is almost certainly no. Due process of law guarantees a basic "fundamental fairness" and typically do not require specific procedures. Courts are in the "interpretation of the law" and the "protecting of constitutional rights" business, not in the "drafting of legislation" business. So do not expect complaints that the legislature would have been better off to draft a law differently to carry much weight with a judge. Challenges to laws and procedures must be serious challenges that allege that a particular law or procedure violates a defendant's constitutional rights and not that those rights would be better protected "if".

> a state rule of law "does not run foul of the Fourteenth Amendment because another method may seem to our thinking to be fairer or wiser or to give a surer promise of protection to the prisoner at bar."

Spencer v. Texas, 385 U.S. 554, 563-64 (1967)

Discretion to Charge Victims and Witnesses

It is not unusual for investigating officers and prosecutors to over look serious criminal conduct of victims and witnesses that are cooperating with the prosecution against a defendant, the more law enforcement or a prosecutor wants to convict a particular defendant the more willing many are to overlook serious criminal conduct of victims and witnesses. The converse is also true, a witness or a victim that is engaged in criminal conduct that is unwilling to cooperate with authorities is much more likely to find themselves charged with a crime. Law enforcement and prosecutors charge uncooperative witnesses in order to gain leverage over them in an attempt to compel the witness's cooperation in the prosecution. There is nothing unlawful or unconstitutional about law enforcement doing this as long as this is disclosed[29] to the defense as required by *Brady v. Maryland*, 373 U.S. 83 (1963) and *Giglio v. United States*, 405 U.S. 150 (1972).

Suspect Interviews

Most often before an investigating officer attempts to interview a suspect, that officer already has probable cause. If an officer already has probable cause before he talks to a suspect and probable cause is all he needs, why is he talking to the suspect? Investigating officers first goal in interviewing a suspect is to get a confession, the backup goal is to tie the suspect down to a story so they can discredit that story. Since a defendant's silence cannot be used against them[30], in most cases a defendant is better off exercising their right to remain silent. Once a defendant starts talking he or she starts giving an investigating officer evidence that can be used to establish probable cause and prepare the case against that defendant at trial.

If a suspect were to decide to give an interview to law enforcement and the suspect gave a really good interview, that interview is not admissible at trial unless the prosecution wants to introduce the statement. Generally speaking, the defense is not allowed to introduce an out-of-court statement of a defendant because it is inadmissible hearsay[31].

---

[29] It will be a question of fact for a jury whether or not a victim or a witness is credible or not.

[30] The use for impeachment purposes of petitioner's silence, at the time of arrest and after they received *Miranda* warnings, violated the Due Process Clause of the Fourteenth Amendment. Post-arrest silence following such warnings is insolubly ambiguous; moreover, it would be fundamentally unfair to allow an arrestee's silence to be used to impeach an explanation subsequently given at trial after he had been impliedly assured, by the *Miranda* warnings, that silence would carry no penalty. *Doyle v. Ohio*, 426 U.S. 610 (1976)

[31] *Williamson v. United States*, 512 U.S. 594, 600 (1994) (the hearsay rule excludes self-exculpatory statements because such statements "are exactly the ones which people are most likely to make even when they are false")

However, if a defendant gives a bad interview that will make them look bad in front of a jury, the prosecution is allowed to introduce the statement. Voluntary statements by a suspect to law enforcement are almost always admissible because they are statements "offered against an opposing party" and were "made by the party" and are not hearsay.[32]

So why should a suspect remain silent? If the statement would help them at trial, their lawyer can generally not get their statement into evidence; and if the statement hurts them at trial, their lawyer will typically not be able to keep it out of evidence. As a general rule, exercising their constitutional right to remain silent is the smartest thing for a defendant to do and experienced criminal lawyers routinely advise their clients to exercise their right to remain silent.

What drives most people suspected of crimes to waive their right to remain silent and give a statement to law enforcement is a fear that if they do not give a statement they will "look guilty" and they will be arrested. In reality, by the time most investigating officers talk to the target of their investigation, they already have everything they need to arrest the target of their investigation and they are just trying to gather enough evidence to ensure the prosecutor can convict the target of their investigation in the event the case proceeds to trial. Frequently, suspects who give statements to law enforcement in hopes of avoiding arrest, give law enforcement enough evidence to convict them.

Another thing people suspected of a crime should know, is that their silence cannot be used against them at trial. However, even a denial may later be used against them. Sometimes out of fear people make blanket denials such as, "I don't know what you are talking about", when they know exactly what the police are talking about. If they later get on the witness stand and testify, they can be impeached with their previous statement. A suspect is much better off not lying to the police, but simply stating "I want to talk with a lawyer and have a lawyer present before answering any questions" and then shut up. Do not ask law enforcement "if" you need a lawyer, tell them you are exercising your right to a lawyer.

---

[32] Fed. R. Evid. 801(d)(2)(A) or in Oklahoma the cite is 12 O.S. § 2801(B)(2)(a)

The Police May Lie

Many people are surprised to learn that the police can lie in order to gain a confession[33]. The police can and do lie to suspects to get them to talk and law enforcement officers are trained to lie to suspects as a strategy.[34] Officers might say things such as they have an eyewitness that can identify the suspect, so the suspect might as well tell them what happened. The police might tell a suspect that they have their fingerprints, DNA or a videotape. If more than one person is arrested they might tell a suspect that the other person has given a statement implicating them. The fact that law enforcement regularly lie to suspects is another reason not to speak with law enforcement if you are a target of their investigation.

Hiring a Lawyer During the Investigation

Hiring a lawyer may be useful to a person who is the target of an investigation by law enforcement, but it is not necessary. An experienced criminal lawyer can help guide the collection and preservation of favorable evidence, advise the potential defendant on what to expect and to advise the defendant regarding any expected charges. Occasionally, a case will come along and an experienced criminal defense attorney will see an opportunity to prevent charges from being filed. Typically, this is not done through dealing with law enforcement, but by dealing with the prosecutor.

Unlike law enforcement who are taught to lie to gain an advantage in questioning a suspect, it is against a prosecutor's ethics to lie.[35] Furthermore, the prosecution is the one that will make the final decision on a case, so it makes sense to speak with the decision

---

[33] See *Frazier v. Cupp*, 394 U.S. 731 (1969); See also *State v. Wakefield*, 267 Kan. 116 (Kan. 1999); See also *Hopkins v. State*, 19 Md. App. 414 (Md. Ct. Spec. App. 1973); See also *Miller v. Fenton*, 796 F.2d 598 (3d Cir. 1986)

[34] If the suspect lies to the officer the suspect is opening themselves up to a charge of obstruction or making a false statement to government officials.

[35] In the course of representing a client a lawyer shall not knowingly:(a) make a false statement of material fact or law to a third person; or (b) fail to disclose a material fact to a third person when disclosure is necessary to avoid assisting a criminal or fraudulent act by a client, unless disclosure is prohibited by Rule 1.6. See Oklahoma Rules of Professional Conduct Rule 4.1 Title 5 of the Oklahoma Statutes

maker instead of law enforcement, if a target of an investigation hires a criminal defense lawyer, the lawyer can communicate directly with the prosecutor.

Gathering Favorable Evidence

It is important for the defense to collect and preserve favorable evidence during the investigatory phase, because some members of law enforcement intentionally do not collect or pursue evidence that is or maybe favorable to the defense, because the prosecution has a duty to turnover evidence that is favorable to the defendant, on both guilt and or punishment ("Brady Material"[36]), or that could be used to question the credibility of a government witness. ("Giglio Information"[37])

---

[36] *Brady v. Maryland*, 373 U.S. 83 (1963)

[37] *Giglio v. United States*, 405 U.S. 150 (1972)

8. Pre-Trial

Arrest

In the criminal justice system the investigation may continue after the arrest, but a defendant is not (or should not be) arrested unless law enforcement believes that they have probable cause that a crime has been committed.

When a person is "arrested on probable cause", they are arrested by law enforcement after the law enforcement has gathered what they believe is enough evidence to establish the defendant has committed a crime. Generally, "probable cause arrest" are felony arrest and not misdemeanor arrest, as a general rule a misdemeanor must be committed in the officer's presence in order for the officer to have the legal authority to make a warrantless misdemeanor arrest[38].

When a person is arrested for a new charge on a warrant, most often law enforcement has finished an investigation, concluded that they have evidence to establish probable cause and submitted that evidence to the prosecution.[39] Then the prosecution has either filed charges against a defendant or submitted the evidence to a grand jury and received an indictment. After formal charges are filed or an indictment is returned a judge will issue an arrest warrant. So when someone is arrested on a warrant, generally the prosecution has already made a decision to prosecute that person.

In some circumstances, when a defendant has been arrested on probable cause, but has not yet been formally charged, there may be a small opportunity to persuade the prosecutor not to file formal charges. However, the majority of the time, once there is an arrest by law enforcement, formal charges are going to be filed by the prosecution.

---

[38] A big exception to this general rule is, misdemeanor domestic assault and battery charges, an officer can make a probable cause arrest for a misdemeanor "Domestic A&B" even if it was not committed in their presence.

[39] When law enforcement concludes that the have probable cause that a crime was committed and they submit that evidence to the prosecution, often times they will submit what is known as an "out of custody affidavit". When an officer makes a "probable cause arrest" before booking the defendant into jail they must complete an "Arrest and Booking" report which will contain a sworn affidavit that includes facts the officer believes will establish probable cause.

Formal Charges

Formal criminal charges are brought by the filing of a "charging instrument". The purpose of a charging instrument is to inform the defendant what they are being accused of, this is part of requirements of "Due Process". In Oklahoma charging instruments must contain "...the title of the action, specifying the name of the court to which the indictment or information is presented, and the names of the parties. A statement of the acts constituting the offense, in ordinary and concise language, and in such manner as to enable a person of common understanding to know what is intended."[40]

In Oklahoma state court formal charges are, almost always, brought by the filing of an "information" and are generally filed by the District Attorney's Office in the county where the crime is alleged to have been committed[41]. In Oklahoma, an "information" will also contain a list of endorsed witnesses and if the state is seeking to enhance the punishment because of the defendant's prior convictions, the "information" will contain a "second page" that alleges the defendant's prior convictions that the state intends on using to seek an enhanced punishment.

In federal court formal charges can either be an "indictment", a "complaint", or an "information". An indictment is formal charges that have been returned by the grand jury. A complaint is a written statement of the essential facts constituting the offense charged that is sworn to in front of a federal magistrate and an information are formal written charges and is used when a defendant agrees to waive an indictment by a grand jury, typically an information is used in federal court in conjunction with plea agreements.

During the investigatory period, the focus had previously been on not giving law enforcement anything that could be used to establish probable cause and collecting favorable evidence law enforcement did not gather that may be needed in case charges were filed. However, once formal charges have been filed the focus of the defense shifts to determining whether or not they can get the charges

---

[40] Title 22 O.S. Section 401

[41] It is possible for the Oklahoma Attorney General's office to also file charges in Oklahoma, but most charges are filed by the local District Attorney's Office.

dismissed and if they cannot get the charges dismissed, on evaluating whether or not they believe the government can prove the charges at trial.

How a defense lawyer attempts to get the charges dismissed will depend largely on the criminal procedure of the criminal justice system the client is charged within. The United States Supreme Court has ruled that probable cause to arrest must be determined by someone independent of the police and the prosecution[42]. However, different jurisdictions make the "independent determination of probable cause" differently. For example, in a system like Oklahoma with an adversarial preliminary hearing process, evidence of probable cause generally must meet the standards of the rules of evidence and is subject to cross examination. In such a system, a defense lawyer will attempt to prevent the state from establishing probable cause by objecting when the rules of evidence are not followed and cross examining the witnesses in an attempt to prevent the evidence from reaching the level of probable cause.

However, defendants that are charged within a system that establishes probable cause through the use of a grand jury, independent probable cause was established when the grand jury returned an indictment and the grand jury's determination of probable cause is generally is not challengeable. If the defense determines that evidence the prosecution used to establish probable cause was obtained in violation of the defendant's rights, the defense may be able to eliminate probable cause with a motion to suppress.

In the vast majority of cases after an independent determination of probable cause has been made, barring some dispositive motion requiring the the dismissal of the charges, the case will either be resolved through a plea or a trial.

Arraignment and/or Initial Appearance

After arrest, an arraignment will be scheduled and the defendant will be informed why the have been arrested and issues such as appointment or entry of counsel, conditions of release, bond, or detention will either be addressed or scheduled for future hearings. If formal charges have been filed and the defendant has a lawyer to

---

[42] *Gerstein v. Pugh*, 420 U.S. 103, 118 (1975) ("that probable cause for the issuance of an arrest warrant must be determined by someone independent of police and prosecution")

represent them, then they can enter a plea of "not guilty" (or "stand mute" and the judge will enter a plea of "not guilty" for them); if formal charges have not been filed or the defendant does not have a lawyer, generally another arraignment or initial appearance will be scheduled. Arraignments[43] are an important part of the criminal procedure because they inform a defendant what crime(s) they have been accused of.

In Oklahoma state court, a defendant can appear for a misdemeanor arraignment through their counsel and their personal appearance is not required[44]. The Federal Rules of Criminal Procedure contains similar language excusing a defendant's personal appearance for an arraignment on a misdemeanor, but requires a written waiver.[45]

There are counties in the state of Oklahoma in a which a judge will enter a plea of not guilty on the defendant's behalf and set the case down some sort of "conference docket" or "attorney status" docket[46]; however, this does not typically occur in federal court.

Determination of Probable Cause

Probable cause protects the people from being arrested, jailed and forced to proceed to trial on unfounded charges, but states are not required to adopt a particular procedure to determine whether or not probable cause exists; as long the procedure they do adopt provides for a fair and reliable determination of probable cause[47]. Some states like Texas use a grand jury system to make a determination whether or not probable cause exist. Other states like Oklahoma primarily use a preliminary hearing system to make the determination of whether or not probable cause has been established. Systems that use a grand jury to determine whether or not probable cause exist, make that

---

[43] See Arraignment of the Defendant Tile 22 O.S. § 451 and Federal Rules of Criminal Procedure 10

[44] Title 22 O.S. § 452

[45] Federal Rule of Criminal Procedure 10(b)(1)(2)

[46] A defendant is only required to have counsel in "critical stages" of the criminal prosecution. A "critical stage" is one that "held significant consequences for the accused." *Woods v. Donald*, 575 U.S. 312, 315 (2015)

[47] *Gerstein v. Pugh*, 420 U.S. 103, 125-126 (1975)

determination before formal charges are filed which means the determination of probable cause is made "ex parte"[48] and the defense generally does not have an opportunity to participate.

In Oklahoma, a defendant charged with a felony, has an Oklahoma Constitutional Right to a preliminary hearing. "No person shall be prosecuted for a felony by information without having had a preliminary examination before an examining magistrate, or having waived such preliminary examination.[49]"

Preliminary hearings are an adversarial hearing in Oklahoma; "The witnesses must be examined in the presence of the defendant, and may be cross-examined by the defendant.[50]"

> At preliminary hearing the State is required to present sufficient evidence to establish (1) probable cause that a crime was committed, and (2) probable cause to believe that the defendant committed the crime. We have recognized that while the State "is not required to prove the defendant's guilt with certainty[,] . . . the State must establish that it is reasonable to believe that the defendant was involved in the commission of the offense." And the State is entitled to the presumption that it will strengthen its evidence at trial. Nevertheless, "the evidence at preliminary hearing must coincide with [the defendant's] guilt and be inconsistent with innocence."
>
> *State v. Heath*, 246 P.3d 723, 725 (Okla. Crim. App. 2011)

If the state is unable to establish probable cause the case is dismissed; however, if the judge presiding over the preliminary hearing determines that they state has established probable cause, the judge will issue a "bind over order", to "bind" a defendant "over for trial".

Preliminary hearings in Oklahoma state court often times become an opportunity for the defense to conduct discovery on cases that they intend to try to a jury. In Oklahoma courts, the state is required

---

[48] One sided

[49] See Oklahoma Constitution Article 2 Section 17

[50] See Title 22 O.S. § 258

to call actual witnesses at a preliminary hearing and is generally not allowed to rely on hearsay[51], which means preliminary hearings are a good opportunity for a defense attorney to elicit favorable[52] testimony from the government's witnesses.

A smart prosecutor will present enough evidence at the preliminary hearing to establish probable cause and no more. During preliminary hearings you often see this tension between the "official" purpose of a preliminary hearing (whether an independent determination of probable cause exist) and the "unofficial" use of the preliminary hearing (as a mechanism for the defense to conduct discovery). Smart defense lawyers have the ability to ask questions, that the answers to, are both relevant to the issue of probable cause and will be useful for the defense at trial. Sometimes you will see lots of objections at a preliminary hearing because the defense is trying to elicit information that will discredit the government's witness at trial and the prosecutor is trying to protect the credibility of their witness.

Sometimes defendants and their families feel like the defense attorney did not do enough to discredit the testimony of the state's witnesses at the preliminary hearing. These are decisions that have to be made by the individual lawyer, sometimes it makes sense to discredit the state's witness at the preliminary hearing and sometimes it does not. For example if by discrediting the state's witnesses at the preliminary hearing the defense lawyer believes that it may create an opportunity to resolve the case without trial, by demonstrating the prosecution's case is not that strong, it may make sense to do so[53]. Additionally depending on the evidence of a particular case and how the defense lawyer is planning on trying the case to a jury, a defense lawyer may want to "lock in" testimony they can use it at trial to discredit the witness. However, in many cases a criminal defense lawyer does not want to let the witness or the prosecution know what is coming at trial, because they feel that their cross examination will be more persuasive if the witness does not know what to expect.

---

[51] Child hearsay is a big exception to this general rule. See 12 O.S. §2803.1

[52] Favorable because it may help at trial.

[53] When a defense lawyer wants to show the prosecution their case is not that strong they are generally maneuvering for a better plea deal.

Most cases that are dismissed in Oklahoma state court, at the preliminary hearing level, are dismissed not because of anything the defense lawyer has done, but because the state is unable to produce the evidence that the state relied upon in arresting and charging the defendant to begin with, typically because of uncooperative witnesses. The most frequently dismissed cases in Oklahoma are domestic violence cases, because complaining witness refuses to show up and the law does not allow for victims of a crime to be arrested as a material witness[54].

Even though the state is required to introduce the actual witnesses and evidence that meets the requirements of the rules of evidence, establishing probable cause is typically not difficult for the prosecution to do in an Oklahoma state preliminary hearing. By the time a case makes it to the preliminary hearing there should have already been a determination that probable cause exist at least three times; once by the officer that made the "probable cause arrest" or conducted the investigation and submitted the "out of custody affidavit" to the district attorney's office, once by the district attorney that determined that probable cause existed and approved the filing of formal charges and once by the judge that either reviewed the "arrest and booking affidavit" from the probable cause arrest or who reviewed the "probable cause affidavit" before signing the warrant. The only difference in determining probable cause at an Oklahoma state preliminary hearing, is that it is an adversarial hearing which allows a defense attorney to object, cross-examine the witnesses, and the evidence submitted at this hearing must meet the requirements of the Oklahoma Rules of Evidence.

Far to often defendants and their families hold false hope that their case is going to get dismissed at a preliminary hearing, when in reality there is little chance of that occurring. Sometimes that "false hope" is nothing more than wishful thinking and other times that false hope is inspired by unscrupulous lawyers that are better at being businessmen, than zealous advocates. Often times these lawyers will

---

[54] "no person may be detained as a material witness to a crime who is a victim of such crime." Title 22 O.S. §720 A; The federal material witness statute does not contain such a restriction on arresting a victim of a crime as a material witness.

withdraw from these defendant's case at the "District Court Arraignment", after being "bound over" for trial[55].

When a defendant has made incriminating statements to law enforcement, statements that establish probable cause, there is a very small chance the case will get dismissed at the preliminary hearing. Why? Because law enforcement is going to show up and tell the judge what the defendant said that established probable cause for the arrest and charges. This is true for any crime that the testimony of law enforcement alone is enough to establish probable cause.

Another feature of the Oklahoma preliminary hearing is that the judges will not make credibility decisions regarding witnesses. The reasoning behind this rule is that credibility decisions are to be made by the jury at trial and not by a judge at a preliminary hearing. I do not personally understand how a court can have a "reasonable person" standard without making some sort of credibility decision, since a "reasonable person" might not believe some of the testimony that occurs at preliminary hearings. However, I can assure you that Oklahoma judges will not make credibility decisions regarding preliminary hearing witnesses and the case law supports their refusal to do so.

In federal courts preliminary hearings are entirely different. Most defendants in federal court are not entitled to a preliminary hearing, because they have been indicted which means the grand jury made the "independent" determination that there was probable cause. When a defendant does receive a preliminary hearing in federal court it is typically nothing more than a formality, because the government is allowed to use hearsay in order to establish probable cause. Federal court defendants are also precluded from challenging the "evidence

---

[55] Hiring a lawyer after a preliminary hearing can be expensive because if a lawyer enters a case after the preliminary hearing, generally the judge will not allow that lawyer to withdraw. This means that the lawyer will have to charge the defendant enough to make it worthwhile if they have to try the case to a jury. It is not unusual to see problems arise between lawyers and their clients over this issue, meaning the lawyer did not charge the client enough to try the case to a jury (or the lawyer does not know how to try the case to a jury) and the client does not want to plea the case. Lawyers have a responsibility to make sure their client understands where they are in a case, but defendants also need to ask the right questions to make sure they understand what their options are.

on the ground that it was unlawfully acquired" at a preliminary hearing.[56]

While the legal purpose of the probable cause protection is to ensure that a defendant is not required to stand trial for a felony offense unless the government has "probable cause", the quality of that protection varies greatly depending on how the system, they are charged within, determines probable cause. In my personal opinion the methods used for the determination of probable cause in the federal system provides little to no protection to defendants, as the old joke goes "you could get a grand jury to indict a ham sandwich."

Remember, unless there is a legal reason to have the case dismissed, once an independent[57] determination of probable cause has been made, a defendant must make a decision of whether they want to plead the case in hopes of reducing punishment or whether or not they want to try the case to a jury.

Motion Hearings

A lawyer can file a motion for anything, Motion to Suppress a Statement, Motion to Suppress a Search, Motion in Limine, Motion for a Bond Reduction, etc. The formula is pretty simple, identify a legal right, give a relevant procedural and factual background, explain the legal right at issue and ask the court to grant appropriate relief. The first thing law students begin learning in law school is "how to think like a lawyer". Lawyers have their own way of thinking about and arguing over legal issues, understanding how lawyers argue is helpful in understanding motions filed in court and opinions issued by courts.

When I attended law school I was taught the **I.R.A.C.** method.

> **I**ssue
>
> **R**ule
>
> **A**pplication
>
> **C**onclusion

---

[56] Federal Rules of Criminal Procedure (FRCP) 5.1 (e)

[57] Remember the requirement for an "independent" determination of probable cause only applies to felonies and not misdemeanors.

Law students are taught how to think like a lawyer through reading judicial opinions to learn how to identify the relevant legal **issues,** the **rule** of law used to decide those issues, how the Court **applied** the rule of law, to reach a legal **conclusion.**

An example of how I.R.A.C. works -
"Theory of Defense Instruction "

Let's say the defendant is on trial (jury trial) for First Degree Malice Aforethought Murder and during the trial, evidence is introduced through the testimony of the defendant that he shot, the alleged victim, because he was in fear of death or serious bodily injury. The defendant's lawyer request that the Court instruct the jury on self-defense. In arguing for the self defense instruction, the defendant's lawyer would analysis the issue similar to this:

I.R.A.C-Trial-Requested Self Defense Jury Instruction

What is the **I**ssue?

Is the defendant entitled to have the jury instructed concerning the right to self defense?

What is the **R**ule of Law?

"As a general proposition a defendant is entitled to an instruction as to any recognized defense for which there exists evidence sufficient for a reasonable jury to find in his favor." *Mathews v. United States*, 485 U.S. 58, 63 (1988) Oklahoma law recognizes self defense as a defense as long as the force used was reasonable and the person was in fear of death or serious bodily injury[58].

Apply the Law to the Facts?

Self defense is a recognized defense, if a person used reasonable force and was in fear of death or serious bodily injury, and the defendant testified that he pointed the firearm because he was in fear of death or serious bodily injury. If the jury were to believe the defendant's testimony and believe the amount of force was reasonable, there is sufficient evidence to find that the defendant was acting in self defense.

---

[58] For the actual instruction see OUJI-CR-8-46

Conclusion

The defendant is entitled to have the jury in his trial instructed upon the law of self defense.

If you pay attention to lawyers arguing in court, lawyers arguing in legal briefs, and court opinions you will see this I.R.A.C. pattern repeated over and over again.

Pleas
Oklahoma State Court Pleas and Sentencing

When pleading a case defendants can enter a plea in their case with a plea agreement or without a plea agreement. Plea agreements in state court most often agree on the sentence, the prosecution and defense will agree to a particular sentence, the sentence will be hand written on the plea form (Form 13.10 Uniform Plea of Guilty - Summary of Facts[59]) and the judge will either accept the plea or reject it.

A plea without a plea agreement is commonly know as a "blind plea" or a "cold plea", which means that the defendant enters the plea of guilty (or some times no contest) and it is up to the judge to determine the appropriate punishment. "Blind pleas" are risky, because a defendant is subjecting themselves to any sentence within the range of punishment and getting such a sentence reversed on appeal is very difficult. ("A sentence within the statutory range will not be modified on appeal unless, considering all the facts and circumstances, it shocks the conscience." *Maxwell v. State*, 1989 OK CR 22, ¶ 12, 775 P.2d 818, 820.)

Sentencing options in state court are relatively simple. Deferred sentence, suspended sentence, split sentence and incarceration. With a deferred sentence the defendant enters a plea and the judge accepts a plea, but the judge does not find the defendant guilty; instead the judges "defers" the sentencing under the conditions of probation. If the defendant complies with the requirements of probation, at the end of the deferred sentence they will be allowed to withdraw their plea and the case will be dismissed. A defendant who successfully completes a deferred sentence will not have a conviction. A deferred

---

[59] This form is used for all felony pleas and misdemeanor charges that serve as a predicate to a felony (Crimes such as DUI and Domestic A & B where the first conviction is. Misdemeanor and the second conviction becomes a felony.)

sentence is like walking right up to the line, but not crossing the line; and as long as the defendant complies with the conditions of probation the case will never turn into a conviction. If the state believes the defendant has violated the terms of the probation, the state will file an application to "accelerate" the deferred sentence.

With a suspended sentence a defendant enters a plea, the judge accepts the plea and finds the defendant guilty and sentences the defendant to jail or prison; however, the judge "suspends" the incarceration portion of the sentence under the conditions of probation. If the defendant complies with the requirements of probation, the incarceration portion of the sentence will never be imposed. Unlike a deferred sentence, a suspended sentence is a conviction. If the state believes the defendant has violated the terms of the suspended sentence the state will file an application to "revoke" the suspended portion of the sentence.

Another sentencing option is a "split" sentence, which means the court imposes both "in time" (incarceration) and "out time" (probation").

Sometimes cases are resolved with a "PSI Rec" or Pre-Sentence Investigation recommendation. What this means is that the parties agree upon the term and whether that term is deferred, suspended or incarceration is left up to the judge, after reviewing a pre-sentence investigation report that is generally[60] prepared by a probation officer for the Department of Corrections. "PSI Recs" are not nearly as common as they used to be.

Sentencing practices for different judges vary widely depending on the judge and or the county.

Federal Court Pleas and Sentencing

Federal court pleas and sentencing is very complicated. Federal courts are much more complicated than state courts in almost every respect. In state court, the plea forms are hand-written on a fill in the blank, pre-printed forms. In federal court, the "Petition to Enter a Plea" form is completed on a computer and generally submitted to the court for review before the "Change of Plea" hearing and a federal plea agreement are frequently more than a dozen pages and will require multiple signatures and initials on every single page.

---

[60] It is possible to get a private PSI report.

Sentencing in federal court always involves a Pre-Sentence Report called a "PSR." In federal court the sentencing is so complicated because of the federal sentencing guidelines. Under the federal sentencing guidelines, each offense has a base offense level, and depending on the offense, there are either enhancements or downward departures. Defendants are generally expected to plead guilty without knowing what the sentence is going to be.

Below is an excerpt, from pages 4 through 5 of the *Petition to Enter Plea of Guilty and Order Entering Plea* for the Northern District of Oklahoma, and is included so you can see just how different sentencing is in federal court.

> I have been advised by counsel that I will be sentenced pursuant to the advisory sentencing guidelines procedure established by Title 18 U.S.C. §3553 et seq. I understand that sentencing is a matter left exclusively in the province of the Court; and I understand that the sentence imposed by the Court may be within the guideline table range provided by law or, for good cause stated, the Court may depart therefrom after all relevant facts and circumstances of my case have been considered by the Court, or the Court may impose a non-guideline sentence.
>
> I further understand that the Court may impose a term of Supervised Release that will run after any term of confinement that might be imposed.
>
> Further, I understand that probation is not available as a sentencing alternative to the Court in most cases under the advisory sentencing guidelines and that, whenever probation is permissible under the advisory sentencing guidelines, it is exclusively within the Court's province to grant or deny probation.
>
> If anyone else, including my attorney, made such a promise, suggestion, or prediction... I know that (s)he had no authority to do so.

In some circumstances, a defendant may be offered a "conditional plea" under FRCP 11 (c)(1)(C). This provision allows the defendant and the government to stipulate to a particular sentence or to particular guidelines. The judge must still accept the plea agreement after the PSR has been prepared. FRCP 11 (c)(1)(C) reads as follows:

...agree that a specific sentence or sentencing range is the appropriate disposition of the case, or that a particular provision of the Sentencing Guidelines, or policy statement, or sentencing factor does or does not apply (such a recommendation or request binds the court once the court accepts the plea agreement).

Often times plea negotiations in federal court involve agreeing to plead guilty to charges without mandatory minimum sentence or with a lower mandatory minimum sentence and then dismissing charges with higher mandatory minimum sentence. After a defendant enters a plea the process of sentencing generally takes a minimum of three months.

9. Analyzing Criminal Cases

Once a criminal case is filed one of three things is going to happen;

1. The case is going to get dismissed.
2. The case is going to be tried to a jury.[61]
3. The case is going to end in a plea of guilty[62] or no contest.

Can I get the Case Dismissed?

The first[63] question a good criminal lawyer considers is "Can I get the case dismissed?" To get a criminal case dismissed either the prosecution has to decide to dismiss the case or there has to be a legal reason for a judge to order the case dismissed. The judge cannot order a case dismissed simply because they do not believe the case should have been filed. (This is a separation of powers issue.) Legal reasons to get a case dismissed generally come down to the prosecution not being able to establish probable cause or the existence of a legal prohibition against the prosecution of the case.

A motion to suppress evidence because of an unlawful search and seizure can sometimes be a legal basis to to get a case dismissed, as long as the evidence is vital to the prosecution's case. For example, if there is an argument that the officer obtained evidence through an illegal search and losing that evidence would mean the government could not establish probable cause, then a motion to suppress could lead to the dismissal of the case.

If the government unlawfully obtained the evidence and raising the issue, will not get rid of the charges, it typically only makes sense to raise the issue in preparation for trial. Why do I say this? If you cannot get the case dismissed even if you win the motion to suppress and you are not willing to try the case to a jury, irritating the prosecution by making them defend a motion to suppress only to turn around and ask them to make your client a favorable plea offer, is a poor strategy.

---

[61] Technically you could try the case to a judge, but that is almost always a bad idea.

[62] Most criminal cases end with the defendant pleading guilty.

[63] If you can get the case dismissed there is no reason to consider whether you could win the case at trial or how you could mitigate the punishment for a case.

It is best to first analyze the case to determine what the goal of the defense is going to be, and to then work towards that goal. If the goal is to work out the best plea agreement possible, fighting the prosecutor over an illegal search, when the prosecution is going to have enough evidence to continue even if you win the motion to suppress, is a bad idea. However, if the defense intends to try the case to a jury, it may make sense to try and get rid of evidence in order to weaken the prosecution's case.

Motions to suppress are most commonly filed in drug cases and other cases involving illegal possession of contraband, but they could also be filed in cases in which the prosecution relies upon a defendant's confession or an identification of a defendant. It is important to keep in mind that just because a lawyer can make an argument does not mean that a lawyer should make the argument. These types of motions should only be filed if there is a reasonable probability of success. It must be understood that if this type of motion is filed and not granted, that it can make plea negotiations more difficult, if working out a favorable plea is the goal.

Additionally, just because there is a good legal argument to support a motion to suppress does not mean that you are guaranteed to win. You should be leery of anyone who is overly confident regarding the chances of winning a motion to suppress. The decision of whether or not to file the motion to suppress may also be influenced by the jurisdiction the defendant is being prosecuted in or the type of charges a defendant is facing. In my experience, motions to suppress are more likely to be granted in federal court than in state court, I suspect because the judges are appointed for life and are insulated from political pressure. It is very difficult to persuade some judges to rule favorably on a motion to suppress, when doing so means the judge must rule that law enforcement officers lied or violated someone's rights. If a case is high profile or a more serious offense, it is also more difficult to get a judge to rule in your favor on a motion to suppress. In my experience it is easier to get a judge to suppress evidence in a minor crime, then a more serious one. I am not saying the law makes it more difficult, I am saying that human nature does[64].

In analyzing a criminal case a good criminal defense lawyer will also ask themselves questions like, "Is there a legal argument based upon a statute or the state or federal Constitution, other than a motion to suppress, that could end the government's case?" Those arguments could take many forms, such as a statute of limitations issue, a legal privilege such as free speech or any argument that would prohibit the government's case from going forward. At this stage of the analysis it is important to keep in mind that we are not talking about arguments and motions that will weaken the government's case, we are talking about a legal argument that would be fatal to the government's case. No, is most often the answer to the question "Can I get the Case Dismissed?"

Based on the Calculation of Risk, Does the Client Want to Proceed to Jury Trial?

If a lawyer cannot get the case dismissed, the next question the lawyer must answer is, "Based on the calculation of risk, does the client want to proceed to jury trial?" Even if a client wants to plead guilty to a case and informs the lawyer they wish to plead guilty, a lawyer should still consider whether or not the prosecution would be able to convict the client at trial. A lawyer has a duty to analyze the case against the client and inform the client if the prosecution may not be able to convict them at trial. Before a client enters a plea and gives up his or her constitutional rights, a lawyer should advise the client of all realistic options.

Calculating the chances of winning a case at trial is the most difficult question to answer when analyzing a criminal case. To properly analyze a criminal case a lawyer must have the jury trial experience to estimate the strength of the government's case, to understand how the evidence will be presented in court, to know what can be brought to light during cross examination, to estimate the credibility of the state and potential defense witnesses and to have a good idea how the evidence will be seen by a jury. A lawyer must consider whether there is a chance of being convicted of a

---

[64] A great book that explains why judges often deny motions to suppress that they should have granted is *Letters to a Young Lawyer* by Alan Dershowitz.

lesser included offense and or what the likely sentence might be if the case is tried to a jury.

Most often times the answer is clear, the government has the evidence to prove the case. If the prosecution has a strong probability of proving its case, and a reasonable plea agreement can be worked out, most defendants should take the deal. Whether or not to take a plea offer is always the defendant's choice and not the lawyer's choice. All a lawyer can do is advise the defendant on what the lawyer believes is the best course of action, it is the defendant's decision whether or not they wish to follow that advice. "Winning at trial" does not have to mean that the defendant is found not guilty. It could mean that the defendant is convicted of a lesser offense or receives a sentence more favorable than the prosecution offers.

If the answer is not clear, or the lawyer believes that there is a reasonable probability of success, then the lawyer along with his client must make the tough decision of deciding whether or not to enter a plea or proceed to trial. In order to make this decision the client must evaluate the calculation of risk.

To properly evaluate the calculation of risk, a client and his or her lawyer, must take into account the chances of winning at trial and consider the risk to the client from a conviction. At first glance one might think that the chances of winning at trial is the same as the calculation of risk, however they are two different things. For example, if a defendant is charged with a misdemeanor DUI and the state has a weak case against the defendant and the lawyer estimates his client has a 70 to 80 percent chance of winning the case at trial, 70 to 80 percent is not the calculation of risk, it is the chances of winning at trial. If the defendant loses and is convicted they could be sentenced up to a year in county jail and lose their job, their car, their house and be unable to support their family. While the chances of winning the case are good (70-80%) the consequences of losing are devastating for the defendant. Not only would the defendant suffer incarceration, the defendant would risk losing everything that they had worked for. Ultimately, it is the defendant's decision, but most defendants facing this scenario would not take the risk of going to trial, despite the good chance of winning at trial.

However, the decision may not be the same if the defendant's personal situation was different. Let's say for example that the defendant was living in the United States and had a green card, and the conviction would result in them being deported. If that was the case, the defendant may decide that the risk was worth it. To properly evaluate the calculation of risk, a lawyer must not only know the legal system well and be able to estimate the chances of receiving different outcomes, but a lawyer must know the client and their personal situation. It is the lawyer's duty to present an evaluation of the case to the client and to discuss with the client the calculation of risk the client faces, but ultimately, it is up to the client to decide whether they want to proceed with trial or to plea the case.

Minimum sentences also influence the calculation of risk. For example, let's say a defendant faces a state first degree murder charge and the state has a very strong case against the defendant, and the lawyer estimates that they have less than a 10% chance of winning the case at trial. In this scenario, the minimum sentence the client will receive if convicted is a life sentence, which means he would be required to serve thirty-eight years and four months (38 and 1/3) before becoming eligible for parole, if the defendant is in their fifties (50s) and the prosecutor is not willing to offer an acceptable plea, the client is almost certainly going to want to take their chances at trial, a defendant in their twenties (20s) may make a different decision.

Defendants may make decisions that the lawyer disagrees with, defendants may even make decisions that most people would consider to be dumb, but that is the defendant's right to do so. The defendant makes decisions based upon their own values, not the values of the lawyer. It is the lawyer's job to analyze and advise the defendant, it is not the lawyer's job to substitute their judgment for that of the client.

How can I Mitigate my Client's Punishment?

If a lawyer cannot beat a criminal case through a motion and it is decided that the calculation of risk makes a trial unwise, a criminal lawyer's focus shifts to mitigation of his client's punishment. Mitigation means the reduction of the seriousness or severity of the sentence that a defendant faces.

Mitigation is a consideration that must be kept in mind during all phases of analyzing a criminal case. For example, in a drug case, if a lawyer files a motion to suppress and fights to have the case dismissed, it may cause the prosecution to be less willing to offer a favorable plea agreement, and that risk should be explained to the client when deciding whether or not to file the motion to suppress.

Plea negotiations are the most common form of mitigation criminal lawyers engage in. Through plea negotiations, lawyers can often work out agreements that mitigate the punishment their clients will receive and limit the risk that they will face.

Mitigation can take many other forms, for example it could be a sentencing brief that explains a defendant's limited mental capacity, personal factors of a defendant that increase the probability of a lenient sentence from the judge, trying the case with the goal of beating the charged offense and receiving a sentence on a lesser offense, or trying the case for punishment.

10. The Jury Trial Process
Pre-Trial Motions

Leading up to a jury trial, both sides have an opportunity to file pre-trial motions which could include motions in limine[65], motions to suppress, requested jury instructions, trial briefs and numerous other motions. Pre-trial motions are generally not dispositive motions, meaning they are not going to determine the outcome of the case, pre-trial motions are typically filed to clarify issues that may arise during trial and to make the trial run more smoothly. Most pre-trial motions pertain to the admission or exclusion of evidence or to jury instructions.

Objections

Objections are a big part of a jury trial, because if the defense counsel does not object and give the judge an opportunity to correct the problem the error is waived for all errors except "plain error[66]". A trial lawyer has a duty to preserve the record and make sure they object to important issues, but that does not mean that a trial lawyer should object to every possible issue. If a lawyer hyperactively objects they lose credibility with the jury because they come across as if they are trying to hide things. To be a good trial lawyer you must also understand appeals, because you need to know what may be important on an appeal and what is not important on appeal, and how to preserve the record in the event their client is convicted.

Good criminal defense trial lawyers must also know both state and federal law, especially United States Supreme Court case law, to properly preserve the record for their clients. The reason United States Supreme Court case law is so important, is because if you are seeking federal review of a state court conviction under federal habeas (28 U.S.C § 2254) one of the ways a defendant can be granted relief is if they can establish the state court appellate opinion, affirming their conviction, was "contrary to, or involved an unreasonable application of, clearly established Federal law, as

---

[65] A "motion in limine" is a motion filed requesting a judicial ruling on an evidentiary issue before it comes up in trial. Motions in Liminie are generally "advisory" which means the issue will typically have to be ruled upon during the trial and a party cannot alone rely upon the ruling on the motion in limine to preserve the record.

[66] *Simpson v. State*, 876 P.2d 690, 693 (Okla. Crim. App. 1994)

determined by the Supreme Court of the United States". If a lawyer does not know United States Supreme Court case law, they do not know when to object or how to preserve the record when they do object.

Just because a lawyer objects during a trial does not mean that the lawyer has properly preserved the record, which largely depends on the basis the lawyer gave for the objection. For example, a lawyer could object to the introduction of evidence based upon "hearsay" and not properly preserve the issue of the introduction of evidence in violation of the defendant's right to confront the witnesses against them[67].

Jury Selection

The beginning of a jury trial is jury selection. How jury selection is conducted will vary from jurisdiction to jurisdiction and from judge to judge within jurisdictions. In some systems the lawyers are very involved in questioning the potential jurors and in other systems the attorneys are not allowed to question the potential jurors[68]. In Oklahoma, both the judge and the attorneys question potential jurors. In my experience in federal court, generally if the attorneys are allowed[69] to question the potential jurors, it is for a very limited time, typically thirty minutes or less.

During jury selection, attorneys are allowed unlimited strikes "for cause" and a limited number of peremptory strikes, a peremptory strike is a strike that excuses a juror from the jury for any reason the

---

[67] Nevertheless, Solomon did not object on Sixth Amendment grounds, and "where a Confrontation Clause objection is not explicitly made below we will not address the constitutional issue in the absence of a conclusion that it was plain error for the district court to fail to raise the constitutional issue *sua sponte*." *United States v. Perez,* 989 F.2d 1574, 1582 (10th Cir. 1993) (en banc). To meet this plain error standard, Solomon must show that the *constitutional* error (1) was obvious, and (2) affected substantial rights. *Id.* at 1583 (citations and quotations omitted). This standard does not apply, however, where the defendant has failed to argue on appeal that the district court committed plain error in not raising the constitutional issue *sua sponte,* as Solomon has failed to do here. *United States v. LaHue,* 261 F.3d 993, 1009 (10th Cir. 2001). We therefore deem the issue waived. *U.S. v. Solomon,* 399 F.3d 1231, 1237-38 (10th Cir. 2005)

[68] The judge is the only person who questions the jurors.

[69] Federal Rules of Criminal Procedure 24 (a)(1) allows for either the judge or the attorneys for the parties to ask questions during jury selection. However, in my experience most federal judges allow very little questioning by the lawyers.

party wants to excuse that juror, except that the peremptory strike cannot be used in a discriminatory manner[70]. In federal court with felony cases, the government is allowed 6 peremptory strikes[71], while the defense is allowed 10 peremptory strikes. In Oklahoma state court, the defense and the state are both allowed the same number of peremptory strikes, 5 for regular felonies and 9 for first degree murder cases[72].

Jury selection is a very important part of the trial and regardless of whether the attorneys have an opportunity to question the jurors themselves or whether the judge handles all of the questioning. The most important thing about jury selection is how the lawyer exercises the preemptory strikes, for a criminal defense trial lawyer to know who to strike and who not to strike, that lawyer must understand their client's case and human nature. This means that the attorney must know the story they will be telling at trial and must have spent the time and effort to think about which type of people will be most receptive to the defense story and who is most likely to reject the defense story.

If the attorney does have the opportunity to speak during jury selection, the attorney needs to keep in mind that not only do the attorneys learn things about the jurors during jury selection, the jurors learn things about the attorney. A lawyer that ask the jurors manipulative questions and attempts to put words into the mouths of jurors during jury selection is damaging their credibility. Credibility with the jury is very important because at the end of the trial the criminal defense lawyer is going to attempt to exchange their credibility for the verdict their client needs.

Opening Statements

During the opening statements both the prosecution and the defense have an opportunity to tell the jury what they expect the evidence to be during the trial. The opening is the first opportunity for the prosecution and the defense to tell the jury their story. During the opening statement, the lawyers should attempt to persuade the

---

[70] *Batson v. Kentucky*, 476 U.S. 79 (1986)

[71] Federal Rules of Criminal Procedure 24 (b)(2)

[72] Title 22 O.S. § 655

jury through storytelling, not argument. Good storytelling can sometimes sound like argument, but there is a difference.

Different jurisdictions have different rules, and judges within those jurisdictions will have different rules for their courtrooms. Some judges limit the length of opening statements and other judges will not. Some judges require that the attorneys stand behind the podium when addressing the jury and other judges permit the attorneys to wander about the courtroom. I am of the opinion that it really does not matter what a judge's rules are for their courtroom as long as they are applied equally to both sides.

Witnesses

After the opening statement, the prosecution begins presenting the government's witnesses and evidence to the jury. The side who calls a witness to the stand will conduct a "direct examination" of that witness. Exhibits are generally introduced through witnesses who can explain to the jury what the exhibits are. Any party can introduce exhibits through any witness as long as the evidence is otherwise admissible and the witness has personal knowledge of the exhibit. A lawyer questioning a witness during direct examination is generally only allowed to ask "non-leading" questions, unless the witness is a hostile witness.

After the "direct examination," the side or sides that did not call the witness will have an opportunity to "cross examine" the witness. One of the most valuable rights a defendant has is the right to "confront"[73] the witnesses against them. Some important cases on confrontation are *Crawford v. Washington*, 541 U.S. 36 (2004), *California v. Green*, 399 U.S. 149 (1970), *Bruton v. United States*, 391 U.S. 123 (1968), *Davis v. Alaska,* 415 U.S. 308 (1974), *Davis v. Washington*, 547 U.S. 813 (2006), *Bullcoming v. New Mexico*, 131 S. Ct. 2705 (2011), *Melendez–Diaz v. Massachusetts*, 557 U.S. 305 (2009) and *Pennsylvania v. Ritchie*, 480 U.S. 39 (1987).

A criminal defense attorney needs to strike hard blows, and not come across as a whiner. Cross examination is one of the most difficult things to do without looking foolish and losing credibility with the jury, keep this in mind if you are "asking" or "insisting" your

---

[73] Cross examination is "greatest legal engine ever invented for the discovery of truth" *California v. Green*, 399 U.S. 149, 158 (1970).

lawyer ask a specific question of a witness. For the defense, the object of cross examination is to influence how the jurors perceive the testimony of the witness, so that the defense has a greater chance of victory with the cross examination than they would have without it, asking one bad question can ruin an otherwise good cross examination.

The process of direct and cross examination continues until the prosecution has presented all of the prosecution's witnesses and evidence. Once the prosecution is done presenting its witnesses and evidence the prosecution "rest," then the defense has the opportunity to present the witnesses and evidence; however, it is not unusual for an experienced criminal defense trial lawyer to call no witnesses because they have proved the defense case in the government's "case in chief". Under some circumstances the prosecution may be allowed to call rebuttal witnesses, and the rules for calling rebuttal witnesses vary from jurisdiction to jurisdiction.

A Defendant's Right to Testify (Or Not Testify)

A defendant has a constitutional right to testify and a defendant had a constitutional right not to testify, these are the defendant's rights and nobody can make this decision for the defendant[74]. Not only does a defendant have a right not to testify, the defendant's decision not to testify[75] cannot be used to imply or argue their guilt. (See *Griffin v. California*, 380 U.S. 609 (1965))

Right to Present a Defense

Another important jury trial right is the right to present a defense. Some important cases on the right to present a defense are *Holmes v. South Carolina*, 547 U.S. 319 (2006), *Crane v. Kentucky*, 476 U.S. 683 (1986) and *Washington v. Texas*, 388 U.S. 14 (1967).

---

[74] See OUJI-CR-9-41-A defendant who wishes to testify is a competent witness. The defendant's testimony is to be judged in the same way as that of any other witness; and OUJI-CR-9-44-The defendant is not compelled to testify, and the fact that a defendant does not testify cannot be used as an inference of guilt and should not prejudice him/her in any way. You must not permit that fact to weigh in the slightest degree against the defendant, nor should this fact enter into your discussions or deliberations in any manner.

[75] A defendant's post arrest silence cannot be used against them. *Doyle v. Ohio*, 426 U.S. 610 (1976)

Jury Instructions

Jury instructions are very important because the jury instructions explain to the jury what the law is and how it should be applied to the evidence. Most jurisdictions have "uniform jury instructions" or "pattern jury instructions". Oklahoma has "OUJIs" or "Oklahoma Uniform Jury Instructions" that have been created by a committee and approved by the Oklahoma Court of Criminal Appeals. Most federal circuits have "pattern jury instructions". It is the lawyer's responsibility to request jury instructions that are necessary for his client to receive a fair trial, and the "uniform" or "pattern" jury instructions are a great place to start. However, just because there is not a "uniform" or "pattern" jury instruction does not mean the defense is not entitled to an instruction, and depending on the legal issue and the evidence a defendant may be entitled to a "theory of defense" instruction. (See *Mathews v. United States*, 485 U.S. 58 (1988))

Two other important issue relating to jury instructions is that the jury decides the issues essential to the defense, not the judge. (See *United States v. Gaudin*, 515 U.S. 506 (1995)) and the judge is required to instruct the jury (when requested[76]) that the defendant is presumed innocent. (See *Taylor v. Kentucky*, 436 U.S. 478 (1978))

Closing Arguments

Each side has an opportunity to give a closing argument and since the prosecution "has the burden of proof" they are allowed both the first and last closing argument. Personally, I think allowing the prosecution the first and last closing argument is unfair and most criminal defense lawyers I know disagree with the practice; however, my opinion on this issue does not matter because the practice of allowing the prosecution the first and last closing arguments is codified in the Federal Rules of Criminal Procedure, Rule 29.1 and in the Oklahoma Statutes, Title 22 O.S. § 831 (6).

During closing arguments, the attorneys are allowed to "argue" the evidence in the case, unlike during opening statements. Different jurisdictions have different rules regarding closing arguments.

---

[76] In most jurisdictions the standard jury instructions tell the jury the defendant is presumed innocent.

Federal courts are typically more strict regarding arguments and time allowed to make them than state courts.

Verdict

After the closing arguments the jury retires to deliberate on a verdict. In federal courts and most state courts the verdict must be unanimous[77]; in Oklahoma the verdict must be unanimous.

---

[77] *Ramos v. Louisiana*, 140 S. Ct. 1390 (2020)

11. Defending Criminal Charges at a Jury Trial

Most criminal cases are resolved by the defendant entering a plea, as they should be. For the vast majority of criminal defendants, trying their case to a jury is a bad idea. The decision to proceed to a jury trial is a serious one and should not be undertaken lightly. The decision to proceed to a jury trial is generally the right decision only when a defendant has the right set of facts, a legal path to victory at trial, a trial lawyer, and no other good choice.

In the dissenting opinion in *Johnson v. Louisiana*, Justice Douglas wrote:

> Any person faced with the awesome power of government is in great jeopardy, even though innocent. Facts are always elusive and often two-faced. What may appear to one to imply guilt may carry no such overtones to another. Every criminal prosecution crosses treacherous ground, for guilt is common to all men.

Johnson v. Louisiana, 406 U.S. 356, 392 (1972)

Most criminal cases that proceed to trial are serious cases in which the prosecution is not offering the defendant much of a choice and therefore trying the case to a jury makes sense from a calculation of risk standpoint. Calculating the risk of a trial is not like calculating the risk of losing a bet; if you loose a bet you lose the money you risked on the bet, if you lose a criminal trial most often you lose your freedom and everything you own.

If possible, defendants who are charged with serious offenses should hire an experienced criminal trial lawyer[78] to represent them. A jury trial is a war and if you are going into a war, you better find yourself a warrior. Few lawyers truly understand what it takes to successfully defend someone accused of a serious crime in front of a jury. A good criminal trial lawyer frequently has the facts against them, the law against them, the police, prosecution, the public and sometimes even the judge against them and they will still fight, scratch and claw to find a way to win. This is not to say that good

---

[78] Not all doctors are surgeons, not all pilots are fighter pilots and not all lawyers are trial lawyers. Finding an experienced criminal trial lawyer may take a little effort on the part of the defendant and his family.

criminal trial lawyers win more than they lose, the system is not set up for the defense to win, but good criminal trial lawyers give their clients a fighting chance.

Just as considering how a potential juror views the power structure and how that relates to the case, the lawyer's view of the power structure also influences their ability to fight the case. I have seen many defendants hire a lawyer for their "connections" to the prosecutor or the judge only to find out that their lawyer does not seem to fight very hard. It's hard for a lawyer to fight the system, if they want be part of it. This is why many defendants with unpopular cases, in small towns, hire out of town lawyers. From time to time a lawyer will encounter a judge that does not want his or her client to receive a fair trial; when a lawyer encounters such a judge, is the lawyer going to stand up and fight for their client or standby and watch their client get railroaded?

Skirmishes In The Culture War

In practice, jury trials are about more than the guilt or innocence of the accused and are not simply a legal process by which a jury weighs the evidence to determine whether or not the government has met the burden of proof, criminal jury trials are skirmishes in the culture war.

Who the defendant is, who the alleged victim is, and who the members of the jury are, is often times just as important as the evidence the government introduces against the accused at trial. We all see the world through the prism of our life experience, and a real criminal trial lawyer understands how political and cultural points of view, influence how jurors weigh the evidence to reach their verdict[79]; this is part of the protection of the right to trial by jury, because it requires those within the "power structure" to prove the case to a jury composed of average members of the community.

Those who doubt that "criminal jury trials are skirmishes in the culture war" should spend some time thinking about some of the high profile criminal cases which have divided our country, along political and ideological lines. Cases like O.J. Simpson, Kyle Rittenhouse, George Floyd, Rodney King, Trayvon Martin (George Zimmerman)

---

[79] "[i]t is part of the established tradition in the use of juries as instruments of public justice that the jury be a body truly representative of the community." *Taylor v. Louisiana*, 419 U.S. 522, 527 (1975)

and the Donald Trump criminal cases. If criminal jury trials are only about applying the law after "weighing" the evidence, why did these cases divide the country along political and cultural lines?

These cases do not represent a new phenomenon, this phenomenon has always existed and is proven in historical cases such as the Scottsboro Boys where nine African-American teenagers in Alabama were accused of raping two white women in 1931 or the trial of Socrates where Socrates was convicted and sentenced to death in 399 BC for impiety against the gods of Athens and corrupting the youth.

Why Trials Become "Skirmishes In The Culture War"

There are differences in the way that individuals that occupy positions of power within the criminal justice system see the world and the way that average people see the world. Because lawyers are typically more liberal[80] than the general population, often times the issues[81] the prosecutors are "out of touch with" the community about, break along political and or socioeconomic lines.

Many[82] of the lawyers involved in the criminal justice system are elitists, I like to say that "they are born on second base and thought they hit a double." These elitists do not see the world the way the average person sees they world[83], but their world view will be reflected in the decisions they make within the criminal justice system. The criminal justice system also attracts people that believe they "know" how society should be organized, but their views are frequently out of alignment with the views of the general public that will make up the jury. I am not saying this to attack prosecutors and law enforcement, I am just trying to explain how the criminal justice system actually works, and to understand why the system sometimes works the way that it does, you need to understand that many people in positions of power within the criminal justice system, see the world differently than the average citizen does.

---

[80] People are frequently surprised to learn that many prosecutors are liberal.

[81] Frequently issues such as self-defense, accusations of rape, accusations regarding child sexual abuses, and spanking and child rearing to name a few.

[82] "Many" but not all.

[83] Ronald Reagan famously said: "The nine most terrifying words in the English language are: 'I'm from the government, and I'm here to help.'"

Let me explain it this way, if I were a school teacher and I had to leave the classroom for a few minutes and I asked my students for volunteers to monitor the class while I was out of the classroom, the student that was most excited about doing that job, is not the one I would pick. Why? Because if they were "too excited" about being a classroom monitor, I would be concerned that they wanted power over the other students, because they enjoyed having power over others. Have you ever wanted to ask a person "Why are you so interested in telling me what to do?" There are a lot of those "types" of people within the criminal justice system, it is a self-selecting group.

If a prosecutor or an officer is an elitists, enjoys having power over others just a little "too much" or is both an "elitist" that also enjoys having power over others just a little "too much", this will influence the way they see a particular criminal case and how they interpret the evidence. Why? Just as the jurors see the world through the prism of their life experiences, these prosecutors and officers see the world through their own.

When a defendant does not like the prosecutor's recommendation and is considering taking a case to jury trial, the question the defendant needs to ask themselves is "Am I seeing this case wrong or is the prosecutor seeing this case wrong?" In my experience, it is generally the defendant that is seeing the case wrong, but there are lots of cases, where it is the prosecutor.

The "skirmish" is between how those within the "system" or the "power structure", "see the evidence and believe it should be interpreted" and how average people "see the evidence and believe it should be interpreted." This is a reflection of the brilliance of the United States Constitution and the separation of powers: that a group of average citizens with no legal training or experience can tell those within "the power structure" that they are wrong, and set the accused free[84]. This is part of the reason why I love being a trial lawyer.

There is frequently an ongoing debate within a society regarding the fairness of that society's criminal justice system; those who are in

---

[84] At its core, the criminal justice system is the enforcement arm of the ruling class and it always has been; and the right to trial by jury is an important limitation on that power. Before the government can convict and send someone to prison, they have to get a jury of average people to agree.

or identify with the power structure of that society believe and argue that the criminal justice system of that society is fair and makes its decisions based upon the rule of law and evidence; people that are not within the power structure frequently argue that the criminal justice system of that society is not fair and makes its decisions based upon biases and prejudices. Since hypocrisy is so much a part of the human condition, it is easy for both sides to point out the hypocrisy of the other side, while being blind to their own.

I am not saying that the majority of people arrested and prosecuted by the criminal justice system do not deserve to be arrested and prosecuted, society has a right to defend itself and its citizens from those that would do them harm, I am writing about this to make this very important point about criminal jury trials, the most important characteristic in selecting a juror for a criminal jury trial is how does that juror view the power structure in that community and how does that view relate to the trial of that criminal case[85]. A lawyer needs a different type of juror if defending a protestor accused of assaulting an officer than that lawyer would need if defending an officer accused of assaulting a protestor; a lawyer who does not understand this, is not a criminal trial lawyer and has no business defending people accused of crimes in front of a jury.

It is because "criminal jury trials are skirmishes in the culture war," that a lawyer needs different types of jurors depending upon "who the client is" and "who the victim is," and all successful criminal defense trial strategies begin with understanding this truth. A real trial lawyer must have the ability to predict with a reasonable degree of certainty, how people from different points of view will see a particular set of facts, because this understanding will influence that lawyer's entire trial strategy.

With an understanding of "who the client is", "who the victim is", and how people with different points of view within that community will view the facts of the case: a good criminal defense trial lawyer uses the facts of the case as building blocks to tell a story the lawyer hopes will persuade the jury to return the verdict that the client needs. A trial lawyer attempts to persuade the jury by using the

---

[85] It is also important to consider how the lawyer views his or her relationship with the power structure. In my opinion it is very difficult for a lawyer that identifies with the power structure to fight the power structure on behalf of his client.

evidence to tell a story designed to appeal to the jurors based upon how those jurors view the world. A trial lawyer is attempting to tell a story that affirms the strongly held beliefs of the members of the jury, because ultimately the story is about the jurors not the client.

During the trial a good trial lawyer will tell the story from his client's perspective so that those that may empathize with his or her client will do so; however, before finishing their closing argument, they will tell their client's story in a way that makes the jurors the hero of of the story for returning the verdict their client needs, the jurors become the hero of the story because their verdict affirms what they believe represents right and wrong.

Criminal Defense Trial Lawyers

A jury trial takes place at the intersection of the legal world and the real world and the world of a jury trial is different than both of them. A criminal defense trial lawyer must know the law, understand human nature and have the oral advocacy skills to present the evidence and tell the story in a compelling way so that the jury will return a favorable verdict. The legal system uses a different form of reasoning than normal people and a good criminal trial lawyer must be fluent in both legal reasoning and human nature; this is partially why there are few good criminal trial lawyers around, simply put most lawyers are not willing to devote the years of time and effort required to become a skilled trial lawyer.

Retired United States District Judge Mark W. Bennett wrote an article titled Eight Traits of Great Trial Lawyers: A Federal Judge's View on How to Shed the Moniker "I am a Litigator"[86]:

> During my time as a federal trial court judge, I have identified ... eight traits of highly effective trial lawyers: (1) unsurpassed storytelling skills, (2) gritty determination to become a great trial lawyer, (3) virtuoso cross- examination skills, (4) slavish preparation, (5) unfailing courtesy, (6) refined listening skills, (7) unsurpassed judgment, and (8) reasonableness. By mastering these, one can become a feared and admired trial lawyer.

---

[86] https://www.mow.uscourts.gov/sites/mow/files/1_Judge_Bennett_8_Traits.pdf

Judge Bennett identified "unsurpassed storytelling skills" as the number one trait of a "Great Trial Lawyer" and I agree with the judge's conclusion that great trial lawyers posses great story telling skills. But, I would explain how someone becomes a trial lawyer a little differently than Judge Bennett. It all begins with a "gritty determination to become a great trial lawyer", because without that desire and determination a lawyer will give up long before they become a "great trial lawyer". Trial lawyers are craftsmen and those that become trial lawyers develop that level of skill and ability, because they pursue it and are determined to have it over the course of many years. The "unsurpassed storytelling skills", "virtuoso cross-examination skills", "refined listening skills", "unsurpassed judgment" and "reasonableness" all develop over the years as a result of their pursuit, which is fueled by their "gritty determination." A trial lawyer has "virtuoso cross- examination skills" because they have developed "refined listening skills," "unsurpassed judgment" and "reasonableness;" which are some of the qualities required to be great at cross examination[87].

A trial lawyer can do things in the courtroom that other lawyers cannot, only because they have spent years and years developing their skill as a trial lawyer. The reward that comes from being a trial lawyer comes at a price and only those that are willing to pay that price will achieve that level of skill and ability.

A Story War

Juries do not use the "facts," "evidence", or "law" to arrive at their verdict; they use stories to arrive at their verdict. While the facts of a case are important, the nature of psychological life is not fact, but story, and stories are uniquely important to human beings. Stories are how humans make sense of the world around them, facts alone are always out of context, it is the story that is important[88].

---

[87] Cross examination is ""greatest legal engine ever invented for the discovery of truth" *California v. Green*, 399 U.S. 149, 158 (1970) and no one can be a great trial lawyer without being a great cross examiner, because without being great at cross examination that lawyer will not be able to extract the evidence that lawyer needs to tell the "great story" or discredit the testimony that would undermine the "great story" they are trying to tell.

[88] I learned this articulation of this idea from former University of Oklahoma Professor Gary Holmes, who was explaining another professor's work.

A lawyer can know every fact about a criminal case and still not know the truth of the case. Ernest Hemingway wrote "All you have to do is write one true sentence. Write the truest sentence that you know." But, Hemingway wrote fiction, what is he talking about when he says "write the truest sentence that you know?" The truth about what? The truth about life, the truth about human nature, the truth about society, the truth about the human experience; that is what makes a great story.

Jury trials are story wars, story telling in a hostile environment. The prosecution is telling one story and the defense is telling another, while both sides do their best to tear apart their opponent's story. A lawyer who does not understand that a jury trial is a story war does not understand the psychological ground rules of a jury trial. Why are great trial lawyers great storytellers? Because being a great storyteller is one of the requirements of being a great trial lawyer.

The criminal justice system allows the jurors to determine what the "facts" of the case are and apply those facts to the law as instructed by the judge. In normal story telling the "facts" as told by the storyteller are accepted as true, this is not the case in the hostile story telling environment of a jury trial. The facts are "determined" by the jury after weighing the evidence and the testimony presented during the trial; a great trial lawyer sculpts the testimony of the opposing witnesses through skillful cross-examination. The "facts" as "found" by the jury does not mean that is "what actually factually occurred", if we could agree on "what actually factually occurred" we would not need a jury most of the time. "What actually factually occurred" is often unknowable, the jury's verdict is based upon the story the jurors believe. Human nature and the human decision making process, dictates that jurors are going to arrange the facts into a story, either one a lawyer has told them or one they come up with on their own.

Developing a Theory of Defense

The first step in developing a story a trial lawyer hopes will persuade the jury to return the verdict his or her client needs is to determine the theory of defense (or their client's legal path to victory[89]); meaning based upon the crime their client is charged with, what the government is required to prove and the available evidence in the case, what is the legal theory that could potentially lead to victory at trial? Once the lawyer has determined the theory of the defense they need to make sure that their client is in agreement with them. If there is no a legal theory (and true facts that support that theory) that could potentially lead to a victory at trial, the lawyer needs to have a conversation with their client about why they are trying the case to a jury.

Developing a theory of defense is done by analyzing the crime the client is charged with, determining what the prosecution is required to prove, reviewing the evidence and making an initial[90] assessment of whether the prosecution has enough evidence to convict. Included in that analysis the lawyer must consider affirmative defenses[91], lesser included offense[92] and the ranges of punishment.

Examples of common affirmative defenses are self-defense, defense of another and entrapment. Available lesser included offenses will depend on the crime charged, the facts of the case and the law of the jurisdiction the defendant is charged in, for first degree murder often[93] times manslaughter is a lesser included offense. Since a trial lawyer is preparing to try the case to a jury, they should generally

---

[89] The theory of defense does not have to include a "legal defense", it could be as simple as the witness is untruthful. For example, "This case is about a girl that told a lie to get out of trouble, and the lie grew too big for her to take it back." A good question to answer in developing a theory of defense is "How could my client find themselves in this situation, and still be not guilty?"

[90] Assessments often changes as the available information changes.

[91] An affirmative defense is a defense that the defendant is required to introduce some evidence of into the record, after which the burden shifts to the prosecution to disprove the affirmative defense.

[92] A lesser included offense is an offense the commission of which is necessarily included in the crime(s) charged. You may also find the defendant guilty of an attempt to commit the charged crime or of an attempt to commit any included crime.

[93] Lesser included offenses are fact and law specific and require careful legal research, especially when you are basing your trial strategy on the lesser included offense being available at trial.

start with the jury instructions or what they expect the jury instructions to be. For example, for a defendant charged with first degree malice aforethought murder in Oklahoma, the prosecution is required to prove the following:

OUJI-CR 4-61[94]

MURDER IN THE FIRST DEGREE

WITH MALICE AFORETHOUGHT - ELEMENTS

No person may be convicted of murder in the first degree unless the State has proved beyond a reasonable doubt each element of the crime. These elements are:

<u>First</u>, the death of a human;

<u>Second</u>, the death was unlawful;

<u>Third</u>, the death was caused by the defendant;

<u>Fourth</u>, the death was caused with malice aforethought.

In analyzing the case to determine whether or not the client has a legal path to victory, the lawyer has to look at the facts of the case and the law. If a lawyer is representing a client who claims he did not cause the death of the person he is being accused of killing (because the police arrested and the prosecution charged the wrong person), the defense of that client would involve fighting to stop the prosecution from proving the third element of Murder In The First Degree With Malice Aforethought ("<u>Third</u>, the death was caused by the defendant;").

Once the lawyer understands how they are going to defend the case from a legal point of view, they must start the process of building the jury trial defense by learning the case so well that they can state a short summary of the theory of defense. That short summary is not stated in technical legal language, but in everyday straight talk. Once the lawyer can state the "theory of defense" in a single sentence, then they begin to build the defense story around the theory of defense, which is the beginning of the process by which a trial lawyer converts the legal defense to a defense that will be presented to the jury.

---

[94] This is the Oklahoma Uniform Jury Instruction "OUJI" for Murder in the First Degree Malice Aforethought.

If stated to a judge, the legal defense would sound something like "The prosecution has failed to prove the third element of murder, 'the death was caused by the defendant' "; but to a jury that legal defense is converted to something like, "Mr. Jones is an innocent man, a victim of mistaken identity," "Mr. Jones is not a killer, he is a victim of a rush to judgement" or perhaps "Mr. Jones was falsely accused because of sloppy police work."

Or perhaps the client admits that he caused the death, but claims he was in fear for his life and acting in self-defense, which means the defense lawyer would be fighting to stop the prosecution from proving the second element of Murder In The First Degree With Malice Aforethought ("<u>Second</u>, the death was unlawful"). With a self defense case the lawyer may write a short summary such as, "Mr. Jones acted in self-defense when he shot _____," " _____ left Mr. Jones no other choice but to use deadly force to defend himself," or "Mr. Jones never thought he would find himself in a kill or be killed situation."

This is the beginning of the "story war" the translation of lawyer talk into real talk and a trial lawyer will take the "theory of defense" and build an entire story around it. Once a lawyer identifies his client's legal path to victory, the lawyer builds the trial defense around that path. If a question, a piece of evidence, an argument or a part of the story does not advance the client down that path to victory, cut it out and get rid of it.

When a trial lawyer presents the client's story to the jury, he or she will use their ability in the courtroom to disrupt, discredit, and undermine the prosecution's story and credibility. For the jury's benefit, the only thing for a criminal defense trial lawyer to talk about is the client's story, anything that interferes with the prosecution's story and anything that the prosecution or their witnesses are trying to hide or lie about.

At the same time a trial lawyer is staying focused on winning the trial, the lawyer must also make a record for an appeal. A trial lawyer must object to preserve errors that interfere with fairness of the trial process without appearing to hide things from the jury, a lawyer who objects hyperactively risk losing credibility with the jury and hurt the client's chances at victory.

Reasonable Inferences

The prosecution is not required to accept the defense's version of events and the defense is not required to accept the prosecution's version of events[95]. When the defense and the prosecution cannot decide upon the "facts" of a criminal case, the dispute is resolved by a jury. Lawyers are never justified in presenting false evidence at a trial: however, lawyers are allowed to use the evidence in a trial to argue "reasonable inferences from the evidence". Consider the drawings below:

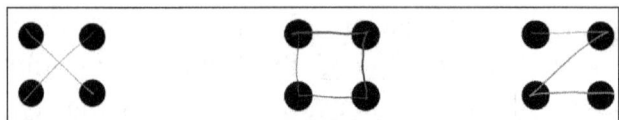

The dots represent the evidence (or facts) presented at trial and the lines represent the reasonable inferences (or stories) from the evidence created by the lawyers. Do the dots represent an "x", "a square" or a "z"? That, is a question of fact for the jury.

A trial lawyer uses the evidence (the facts) as building blocks for the inferences they want to create in the minds of the jurors to build the defense story. It is the story told from the facts that matter, everyone talks about the "evidence" in a trial, but few people talk about the story. Just as all painters start with a blank canvas, paints and a brush; they create different pictures depending on what they include and exclude and how the use their brush to fill the canvas. There is an art to being a trial lawyer, and different lawyers see cases differently and present the case differently just as different artists paint different pictures.

It is the ability of the trial lawyer to understand their client's story, to understand human nature and to paint a favorable picture of the story they are telling in minds of the jurors that matters; this is a true mark of a trial lawyer and you cannot be a trial lawyer without that ability. Whether or not the jury believes the prosecution's story, the defense story or comes up with their own story is a "question of fact" for the jury.

---

[95] This is one of the most difficult things for defendants and their families to accept.

For a criminal defense lawyer, trial advocacy is the ability to tell your client's story in a hostile environment and with the deck stacked against your client. Why is the deck stacked against your client? Because you are defending your client against "the awesome power of government".

I have lived my life, and I have fought my battles, not against the weak and the poor—anybody can do that—but against power, against injustice, against oppression, and I have asked no odds from them, and I never shall.

Clarence S. Darrow, *Attorney for the Damned* 491, 497 (Arthur Weinberg ed. 1957).

How can a criminal defense lawyer overcome such odds? By telling his client's story to the right jury. John Truby discusses in the *Anatomy of Story* that there is a dramatic code embedded beneath the surface of the story that carries the moral message to the listener of the story. This is part of the true power of storytelling. Storytelling is hardwired, it is subconscious and a sound trial strategy has to begin with storytelling; because as humans we are hardwired, pre-programmed to receive information through stories, it is part of the human condition.

Famous trial lawyer Gerry Spence said "Tell the story that helps bring the story to the surface for the jury. Find the bad guy and tell the jury about the bad guy first." Great storytelling doesn't just tell the jury what happened from the defendant's point of view, as Spence said it "bring[s] the story to the surface," it gives the experience of what happened; it allows the jurors to relive the events so that they can understand the decisions and emotions of the defendant as he or she lived them. It is not enough to tell the story, the jury must feel the story, they must live the story and experience the story; when they are experiencing the story they are more likely to accept the message of the story. Renowned trial lawyer Jeff Fieger says "it is not a question of telling a story it is a question of believing the story." A trial lawyer has to tell their client's story in such a way that they believe the story they are telling, so they can tap into the true emotions of the story; with the proper emotion the trial lawyer has credibility and trustworthiness, which helps the jurors to be drawn into the story so that they can receive the story's message.

Gerry Spence won cases largely through cross-examination of the government's witnesses. "I am the only one that tells the whole truth...government agents, cops and prosecutors almost never tell the whole truth. If you call witnesses you better tell the whole truth or you will lose credibility with the jury...tell the relevant part of your client's story on cross examination...cross examination is another opportunity to tell your client's story."

A trial lawyer cannot tell the jury everything; they must leave things for the jury to figure out on their own, the "figuring out part" of the story is part of what draws the jury into the story. While a defendant needs to tell his lawyer everything, a defendant should not insist that his or her lawyer "tell the jury everything", because if you tell the jury everything you will not draw them into the story. Additionally, if the jury (or juror) reach a conclusion on their own, they will not let go of it as easily as they would, if one of the lawyers told them the conclusion they should reach, a lawyer has to trust the jurors to reach the right conclusion and leaving things for the jurors to figure out is part of trusting the jurors.

The fuel for the story is tension, tension is created by juxtaposing two contradictory ideas next to each other. Chronological stories with too many details typically fail, because there are too many details separating the facts that build tension. As a trial lawyer you can always fill in the "details" during the trial or allow the "details" to be part of the "figuring out part". In telling the story to the jury, if it is not necessary to understand the story or does not build tension, cut it out. If there is a fact that has to be told to the jury, a bad fact, do it in such a way that builds tension. Whatever you are trying to convince the jury of is something you should build tension around; desire makes great tension so the jury understands the motivations (or intent) and that will help hold the story together.[96]

Paul Luvera, a trial lawyer and a member of the American Trial Lawyers Hall of Fame, says "we should capture the hearts of the jurors by storytelling. Make stories interesting, short, simple and compelling. Trials are battles of impressions and not logic."

---

[96] Sequence of events and causal connections is what holds a story together. Motivation, desire or intent make great causal connections in jury trial story telling.

Trial lawyers also need to be careful that they do not fall into the trap of feeling that they have to be original or have some unique insight into human nature, as Willa Cather wrote in *O Pioneers!* "There are only two or three human stories, and they go on repeating themselves as fiercely as if they had never happened before."

12. Direct Appeal
How a Conviction Is Obtained Determines How It Must Be Challenged

How a defendant receives a sentence determines how a defendant must challenge that sentence[97]. A direct appeal is an appeal of a verdict (either from a judge or a jury), not an appeal of a plea of guilty or no contest. In Oklahoma, a defendant that does not receive their sentence through a trial, does not file a direct appeal or a "post-conviction", they must file a "motion to withdraw" their plea or a motion to withdraw a plea "out of time." Oklahoma is not unique in this respect; most if not all American criminal justice systems have a different process to challenge a criminal sentence received by a plea, then a sentence received by a trial.

Challenging Sentences Based Upon Pleas

Below is the process to challenge a sentence received after a plea of guilty or no contest. If this sounds familiar, it should, this is printed on the PLEA OF GUILTY- SUMMARY OF FACTS form[98] that is required to be completed for every felony plea in Oklahoma. On the standard Oklahoma plea of guilty form, this is referred to as the "Notice of Right to Appeal" and every defendant that enters a plea of guilty in Oklahoma is required to sign acknowledging that they understand these rights; and their lawyers are required to sign the form attesting that they "...have advised the Defendant of his appellate rights." If you are planning on attempting to withdraw your plea out of time and you do not remember being informed of these rights, I would encourage you to have a friend or family member go to the courthouse and pay for a copy of your PLEA OF GUILTY- SUMMARY OF FACTS form that was used when you entered your plea.

> To appeal from a conviction, or order deferring sentence, on your plea of guilty or no contest, you must file in the District Court Clerk's Office of the court that accepted your plea, a written Application to Withdraw your Plea of Guilty within ten (10) days from the sentencing date. You must set forth in

---

[97] In Oklahoma see Oklahoma Court of Criminal Appeals Rule 2.1

[98] See Form 13.10 Uniform Plea of Guilty - Summary of Facts

detail why you are requesting to withdraw your plea. The trial court must hold a hearing and rule upon your Application within thirty (30) days from the date it is filed. If the trial court denies your Application, you have the right to ask the Court of Criminal Appeals to review the District Court's denial by filing a Petition for Writ of Certiorari within ninety (90) days from the date of the denial. Within ten (10) days from the date the application to withdraw plea of guilty is denied, you must file a notice of intent to appeal and designation of record pursuant to Oklahoma Court of Criminal Appeals Rule 4.2(D). If you are indigent, you have the right to be represented on appeal by a court appointed attorney.

When considering motions to withdraw a plea, the only two things the courts will consider are whether or not the plea was knowingly and voluntarily entered and whether or not the court that accepted the plea had jurisdiction over the charges. If you make a motion to withdraw your plea be sure and explain why it is that your plea, was not knowingly and voluntarily entered or why you believe the court that accepted the plea did not have jurisdiction. (The courts almost always have jurisdiction.)

If you fail to file an application to withdraw your plea within 10 days of the sentencing date, then the law presumes that you waived your right to attempt to withdraw your plea and you must first go through a process to overcome the legal presumption of a waiver. You must file a request "for a recommendation that you be allowed to withdraw your plea out of time" with the trial court. The trial court will consider why it was that you did not file the request to withdraw your plea within 10 days and make a recommendation about whether or not you should be allowed to attempt to withdraw your plea out of time. (The court is considering whether or not you have a good reason for failing to file your motion within the 10 day period.)

You must then file with the Oklahoma Court of Criminal Appeals a Motion to Withdraw Plea Out of Time and attach the trial court's recommendation. Only the Court of Criminal Appeals can grant you the right to file your motion to withdraw your plea out of time. If the Court of Criminal Appeals grants that right, then you go back to the trial court and file your motion to withdraw your plea and the case proceeds in the same manner as if it was filed within 10 days.

If you are successful in withdrawing your plea you are then placed in the same position that you were prior to entering the plea, meaning you are still facing the same criminal charges. If your charges were reduced as part of a plea agreement in all likelihood your original charges will be re-instated.

Limited Ways to Change an Oklahoma Criminal Sentence

There are only six ways to change an Oklahoma conviction (or sentence), using the judiciary[99], once it has been imposed[100]. Other than the six ways listed below, courts do not have jurisdiction (the legal right to act) to modify or vacate a sentence. These ways are:

1. Reversal on Direct Appeal (Applies to trial verdicts, both jury and non-jury)
2. Post-Conviction Relief under Title 22 O.S. § 1080 (Applies to trial verdicts, both jury and non-jury)
3. Federal Habeas for a state prisoner under 28 U.S.C § 2254
4. Withdrawal of Plea either filed in time (Within 10 days of the sentencing) or filed out of time
5. Sentence Modifications under Title 22 O.S. § 982 (a)[101]
6. Oklahoma Survivors Act under Title 22 O.S. § 1090.1 through §1090.5.

In addition to the six ways listed above, the only other way a defendant can get a sentence modified is through executive action, which would be commutation and or a pardon, which is not covered in this book.

---

[99] It may be possible, depending on the law in the jurisdiction of the conviction, to seek a commutation or pardon through the executive branch

[100] As of this writing.

[101] There is a common misconception in Oklahoma prisons that there is a "Motion for a Time Cut" in Oklahoma criminal law, such a motion does not exists. The closest thing to a "Motion for a Time Cut" would be a "motion for a sentence modification" which most people will not qualify for without the agreement of the prosecution (See Title 22 O.S. § 982 (a)).

A Comprehensive Plan for Fighting Trial Convictions

When fighting a conviction received at trial, a defendant or someone representing a defendant needs to look at the case comprehensively and develop a plan to fight the conviction all the way through federal habeas, if necessary. This plan should start before direct appeal when selecting the issues to appeal and writing the brief for the direct appeal, one should make every effort to "federalize"[102] the issues so they can continue to fight the case on federal habeas if possible, without having to go through the state post-conviction relief process. A defendant who exhausts all of their state remedies on direct appeal will generally have a more favorable "standard of review" than a defendant who had to go through the state post-conviction relief process to raise issues that were not raised on direct appeal.

I am not saying a defendant should abandon good issues simply because they were not raised on direct appeal, but I am saying that a defendant generally has a better chance of winning an appeal on federal habeas if the issues were raised on direct appeal in a way that "federalizes" the issues. Generally speaking, the earlier an issue is raised (or objected to) the more favorable the standard of review is for the defendant. This is important in every case, but particularly important when a defendant does not have the financial resources to hire a lawyer to handle their case after direct appeal[103]. (State post conviction or federal habeas case)

Appeals Are About Process, Not Guilt or Innocence

Criminal jury trials are about presenting the evidence and arguments to a jury in a fair manner so that the jury can make a "factual" determination of the guilt or innocence of the accused, but appeals are about the process that was used when the jury convicted

---

[102] You cannot win an appeal in federal court on an issue only based upon state law so the issues must be argued from a position that the Appellant's federal rights were violated.

[103] To have a chance at winning a federal habeas case pro se you must work hard to understand the process and the law and then choose your issues carefully. Additionally, if you successfully make it into federal court on a good issue that the judge believes has merit, federal judges are much more likely to appoint you an attorney than state court judges. But you must learn the law and make every effort to follow the rules, otherwise you are almost certain to be denied.

the defendant[104]. This is the most important thing to understand about appealing criminal convictions based upon verdicts. Once a jury reaches a verdict and convicts a defendant, all of the presumptions shift, and a defendant will never get his or her conviction overturned if they do not focus on the process that was used to reach that verdict.

To win an appeal and reverse a conviction, you must persuade an appellate court that the process by which the jury reached the verdict of guilt was seriously flawed, you meet the applicable "standard of review" for that legal issue, and with most errors you will have to prove that the legal error committed during the trial was serious and likely influenced the outcome of the trial. (The harmless error test)

There is a common misconception regarding criminal law, that many criminal convictions are reversed on "technicalities"[105], nothing could be further from the truth. Errors that did not substantially affect the fairness of the process are know as "harmless error" and will typically not get a conviction reversed. When a criminal conviction is reversed it is almost always reversed because there are serious problems with the process used to obtain that conviction. Do not expect technicalities to reverse your conviction, you must have serious problems that affected the fairness and outcome of your case to get the conviction reversed.

At a jury trial, the jury is the "finder of fact"[106], this means that the jury makes determinations of facts in reaching a verdict of guilt or innocence. Juries make determinations of what evidence they believe and what evidence they do not believe. Appellate courts are not going to replace a criminal jury's determination of fact with its own determination of fact, because that is not the function of an appellate court. The jury judges the facts of a case to reach a verdict, the appellate court judges the fairness of the process used to reach that verdict. An appellate court is not going to assume the fact finding role of the jury, that is not their job. The appellate court's job

---

[104] There is no appeal if the defendant is found Not Guilty because the state cannot appeal. *United States v Ball*, 163 U.S. 662 (1896)

[105] When someone argues the conviction was "reversed on a technicality" they do not like the decision and are trying to discredit it.

[106] There are situations in which the judge makes determinations of fact, this frequently happens in ruling on objections.

is to consider the arguments made by the parties and give an opinion about whether or not the trial process of the case was so flawed that the jury's verdict should be reversed.

Appellate courts will not easily overturn a criminal jury verdict for good reason, our system is designed based upon the separation of powers and the right to trial by jury is an important part of the separation of powers. To win on appeal, in most cases a defendant must convince the appellate court that their rights were violated and that the violation of their rights was serious. With the exception of fundamental (or structural)[107] errors, a defendant bears the burden to prove the error in their trial made a difference in the outcome.

If a state court conviction is "affirmed" on appeal a defendant can appeal the state court opinion affirming their conviction to federal district court. However, to get a federal court to reverse a state court decision, it is even more difficult. First of all you must give the state courts every opportunity that you can to fix the "problem". (This is called exhaustion of state remedies.) Second you can only appeal to federal courts if your federal constitutional rights were violated. You cannot win an appeal in federal court appealing an issue only based upon state law. Third, when using federal habeas (28 U.S.C. §2254), in most cases, you must establish that the state appellate court reached a conclusion that was contrary to clearly established federal law or "unreasonable determination of the facts in light of the evidence presented in the state court proceeding."

Standards of Review

Most people have never heard of the term "standard of review", a standard of review is the legal test that appellate courts use in "reviewing" the decisions of lower courts. Just as a defendant is "presumed innocent" at trial, on appeal it is most often presumed that the decisions made below by the judge and the jury were correct.

---

[107] The purpose of the structural error doctrine is to ensure insistence on certain basic, constitutional guarantees that should define the framework of any criminal trial. Thus, the defining feature of a structural error is that it "affect[s] the framework within which the trial proceeds," rather than being "simply an error in the trial process itself." Id ., at 310, 111 S.Ct. 1246. For the same reason, a structural error "def[ies] analysis by harmless error standards." Id., at 309, 111 S.Ct. 1246 (internal quotation marks omitted). *Weaver v. Massachusetts*, 137 S. Ct. 1899, 1907-08 (2017)

And just as the prosecution has the burden of proving the defendant's guilt beyond a reasonable doubt at trial, on appeal now the defendant has the burden of convincing the appellate court that the decisions made at the trial court level were not only wrong, but were so wrong that the appellate court should grant relief. To win on appeal, a defendant must pay close attention to the standards of review for the issues they are raising.

Throughout the criminal appellate system there are various "standards of review". These "standards of review" are actually nothing more than presumptions and burdens of proof, depending on the situation the presumption will be different and the burden of proof to overcome that presumption will be different.

At a trial, a defendant has the presumption of innocence, and to overcome that presumption of innocence, the state has the burden of proving every element of every offense beyond a reasonable doubt. But once a defendant is convicted, the presumption of innocence is replaced with presumptions that the jury and the trial judge made the right decisions. After conviction, not only is the presumption of innocence gone, but after a conviction the defendant bears the burden of proof, the burden of proving that the process by which the jury reached its decision was seriously flawed.

Often times the appellate court will not use the phrase "standard of review" and will instead say something like "we review trial courts rulings on the admissibility of evidence for....".

Below is a quote from a law review article discussing "Standards of Review":

> It would be difficult to name a significant legal precept that has been treated more cavalierly than standard of review. Some courts invoke it talismanically[108] to authenticate the rest of their opinions. Once they state the standard, they then ignore it throughout their analysis of the issues. Other courts use standard of review to create an illusion of harmony between the appropriate result and the applicable law. If an appellate court wants to reverse a lower tribunal, it characterizes the issue as a mixed issue of law and fact,

---

[108] As it was possessed or believed to possess magic power especially protective power.

thereby allowing de novo review. If the court wants to affirm, it characterizes the issue as one of fact or of discretion. It then applies a higher (more deferential) standard to the lower tribunal's decision. Finally, some courts disregard standard of review in their analysis entirely.

Standard of review has been virtually ignored by legal scholars. The phrase does not even appear in any of the major law dictionaries. Yet, as a concept, it is essential to every appellate court decision. It is to the appellate court what the burden of proof is to the trial court. Ironically, although no trial judge would think of sending a case to the jury without an instruction on the burden of proof, appellate judges often omit the standard of review when they discuss whether or not to overrule a trial court's determination.

(See Kelly Kunsch, *Standard of Review (State & Federal): A Primer*, Seattle University L. Rev. Vol. 18, No. 1, 12 (Fall 1994)).

The standard of review is the test by which the decision of a lower court will be measured by a higher court to determine whether or not to reverse the decision. "Standards of review" are so important that sometimes you will see judges arguing about them in the "majority opinion" and the "dissenting opinion". (For an example of this see *Seabolt v. State*, 2006 OK CR 50, 152 P.3d 235 (Okla.Crim. 2006) see also see *Rea v State*, 2001 OK CR 28, 34 P.3d 148 (Okla.Crim. 2001)) The reason that judges sometimes argue over the proper "standard of review" to apply to a particular issue is because often times it is the "standard of review" that ultimately determines whether or not the appeal will be granted or denied. The justification for different "standards of review" can be found in the limited role the appellate courts are supposed to play in the criminal justice system, in other words, it is a separation of powers issue.

What Are Some Of The Different Standards Of Review?

There are different standards of review and the list below is not exhaustive, each issue must be researched to determine the proper standard of review for that court and the procedural stage of the appeal. The list below gives some examples to help explain the concept so you can identify the standard of review in appellate opinions. Since appellate courts are constantly releasing new opinions, case law is always changing and therefore every legal issue must be researched to make sure the case law has not changed.

De Novo Review

Under "de novo" review, the appellate court gives no deference to the trial court's ruling and considers the issue without any regard for the trial court's decision. "De novo" means "anew", "from the beginning" or "afresh". "De novo" review is the standard that is one of the most favorable to a defendant because the appellate court is not deferring to the lower court's decision. Questions of law are generally reviewed de novo, because the courts of appeals are concerned with defining the law, and they generally do not give deference to the trial court's assessment of purely legal questions.

Abuse Of Discretion

With the abuse of discretion standard of review the appellate court decides if the lower opinion is "unreasonable or arbitrary action made without proper consideration of the relevant facts and law, also described as a clearly erroneous conclusion and judgment, clearly against the logic and effect of the facts." (*Neloms v. State*, 2012 OK CR 7, ¶ 35, 274 P.3d 161, 170.)

Some examples of situations in which an appellate court would apply an abuse of discretion standard are listed below:

A trial court's failure to apply the law correctly in making a ruling is always an abuse of discretion. (See *Koon v. United States*, 518 U.S. 81, 100 (1996); "A district court by definition abuses its discretion when it makes an error of law.").

The extent of cross-examination rests in the discretion of the trial court and reversal is only warranted where there is an abuse of discretion resulting in prejudice to the defendant, this is true as long as the restrictions on cross examination do not implicate the defendant's Sixth Amendment right to confront[109] the witnesses against them. (See *Parker v. State*, 1996 OK CR 19, ¶ 13, 917 P.2d 980, 984, cert. denied, 519 U.S. 1096, 117 S.Ct. 777, 136 L.Ed.2d 721 (1997).

---

[109] Where limitations on cross-examination directly implicate a defendant's Sixth Amendment right of confrontation, the Oklahoma Court of Criminal Appeals will review the limitation using the "de novo" review standard. *(See Scott v. State,* 1995 OK CR 14, ¶¶ 21-27, 891 P.2d at 1292-93*)*

The decision whether to disqualify a prospective juror for cause rests in the trial court's sound discretion, and appellate courts apply an abuse of discretion standard, in reviewing those decisions on appeal. (See *Allen v. State*, 862 P.2d 487, 491 (Okl.Cr.1993), cert. denied, 511 U.S. 1075, 114 S.Ct. 1657, 128 L.Ed.2d 375 (1994) and *Black v. State*, 2001 OK CR 5, ¶ 25, 21 P.3d 1047, 1060.)

The manner and extent of a trial court's voir dire is reviewed by the Oklahoma Court of Criminal Appeals under an abuse of discretion standard and the Court will not reverse unless an abuse of discretion is shown. (See *Littlejohn v. State*, 2004 OK CR 6, ¶ 49, 85 P.3d 287, 301)

The determination of which instructions shall be given to the jury is a matter within the discretion of the trial court. *Cipriano v. State*, 2001 OK CR 25, 714, 32 P.3d 869, 873 (Okl.Cr.2001)

Clearly Erroneous

A trial judge's factual findings are given great deference because the trial judge has presided over the trial, heard the testimony, and has the best understanding of the evidence. This is also true when a trial judge considers evidence regarding pre-trial motions, such as a motion to suppress evidence. Under the clearly erroneous standard, it is not enough to show that the factual decision was questionable. It is very difficult to overturn a trial court's factual determination, so if your appeal rests solely on a challenge to a finding of fact, your likelihood of success will be low, unless the determination was clearly a bad decision.

Insufficient as a Matter of Law

In criminal cases, the due process clauses of the Fifth and Fourteenth Amendments require that criminal convictions be based on sufficient evidence presented at trial. Therefore, an appellate court must reverse a conviction if, after considering the evidence in the light most favorable to the state, it finds no "rational trier of fact could have found the essential elements of the crime beyond a reasonable doubt." *Jackson v. Virginia*, 443 U.S. 307, 319 (1979).

In determining whether or not there was sufficient evidence to convict a defendant at trial, Oklahoma's Court of Criminal Appeals applies the standard of review set forth in *Spuehler v. State*, 1985 OK CR 132, ¶ 7, 709 P.2d 202, 203-204, "whether, after reviewing the evidence in the light most favorable to the prosecution, any rational trier of fact could have found the essential elements of the crime charged beyond a reasonable doubt." A reviewing court must accept all reasons, inferences, and credibility choices that tend to support the verdict. See *Washington v. State*, 1986 OK CR 176, ¶ 8, 729 P.2d 509, 510.

Shock the Conscience

A sentence within the statutory range will not be modified on appeal by the Oklahoma Court of Criminal Appeals unless, considering all the facts and circumstances, it shocks the conscience. *Maxwell v. State*, 1989 OK CR 22, ¶ 12, 775 P.2d 818, 820. To "shock the conscience" has been defined to mean manifestly and grossly unjust.

Plain Error

Plain error[110], or "un-objected to error", is a very important concept to understand on appeal and is applied to and plain error has its own standard of review.

> ...this Court determines whether the appellant has shown an actual error, which is plain or obvious, and which affects his or her substantial rights. This Court will only correct plain error if the error seriously affects the fairness, integrity or public reputation of the judicial proceedings or otherwise represents a miscarriage of justice. Id. *Hogan v. State*, 2006 OK CR 19, ¶ 38, 139 P.3d 907, 923. See also *Jackson v. State*, 2016 OK CR 5, ¶ 4, 371 P.3d 1120, 1121; *Levering v. State*, 2013 OK CR 19, ¶ 6, 315 P.3d 392, 395.

Fredrick v State, 400 P.3d 786 (Okla.Crim. 2017)

Ineffective Assistance of Counsel Standard of Review

Claims of ineffective assistance of counsel are most frequently considered for the first time on appeal and typically have not been raised or ruled upon by the trial court, so defendants do not have to overcome presumptions concerning the trial court's factual rulings.

---

[110] To understand the "plain error" standard better, it will be helpful to read the decisions of *Simpson v State*, 1994 OK CR 40, 876 P.2d 690 (Okla.Crim. 1994), *Bland v. State*, 2000 OK CR 11, ¶ 49, 4 P.3d 702 (Okla.Crim. 2000), *Romano v. State*, 1995 OK CR74, ¶ 18, 909 P.2d 92 (Okla.Crim. 1995) and to read Title 12 O.S. Section 2104.

This is true is because it is typically raised against the trial attorney by the appellate attorney and not by the trial attorney against themselves.

However, ineffective assistance of counsel claims have their own standard of review that with presumptions that weigh heavily against a defendant already built into the presumptions of review. With most ineffective assistance of counsel claims courts do not defer to the findings of the lower court, but to the decisions of the defense counsel. (Courts "indulge a strong presumption that counsel's conduct" was constitutionally adequate and that "judicial scrutiny of counsel's performance must be highly deferential.")

The most often quoted case on ineffective assistance of counsel is the United States Supreme Court case of *Strickland v. Washington,* if you believe that your case may involve ineffective assistance of counsel, I would encourage you to United States Supreme Court cases that cites *Strickland v. Washington.*

In *Jones v. State,* 2009 OK CR 1, 201 P.3d 869 (Okla.Crim. 2009) the Oklahoma Court of Criminal Appeals has a good discussion of ineffective assistance of counsel claims.

> As for counsel's conduct, we review claims of ineffective assistance under the standard set forth in *Strickland v. Washington*, 466 U.S. 668, 687, 104 S.Ct. 2052, 2064, 80 L.Ed.2d 674 (1984). *Warner v. State*, 2006 OK CR 40, ¶¶ 198-199, 144 P.3d 838, 891-892. Strickland sets forth the two-part test which must be applied to determine whether a defendant has been denied effective assistance of counsel. Id. First, the defendant must show that counsel's performance was deficient, and second, he must show the deficient performance prejudiced the defense. Id. Unless the defendant makes both showings, "it cannot be said that the conviction ... resulted from a breakdown in the adversary process that renders the result unreliable." Id. quoting *Strickland*, 466 U.S. at 687, 104 S.Ct. at 2064.
>
> Appellant must demonstrate that counsel's representation was unreasonable under prevailing professional norms and that the challenged action could not be considered sound trial strategy. Id. The burden rests with Appellant to show that

there is a reasonable probability that, but for any unprofessional errors by counsel, the result of the proceeding would have been different. Id. A reasonable probability is a probability sufficient to undermine confidence in the outcome. Id., citing *Strickland*, 466 U.S. at 698, 104 S.Ct. at 2070, 80 L.Ed.2d at 700.

Harmless Error

Harmless error is an important concept to understand in the appeal of criminal convictions. With most errors, the appellate courts also analyze those errors using the harmless error analysis. So when the error is the type of error that must also be analyzed through the harmless error analysis, persuading an appellate court that the trial court committed a legal error and that the error meets the appropriate standard of review is not enough to win a reversal. The defendant must also satisfy the "harmless error" analysis by demonstrating that the error prejudiced to his or her case.

To demonstrate prejudice, a defendant must show that the complained of error "worked to his [or her] actual and substantial disadvantage, infecting [the] entire trial with error of constitutional dimensions." (See *U.S. v. Frady*, 456 U.S. 152, 170 (1982)) To establish prejudice, the applicant will have to establish that but for the error, the outcome would have likely been different. (See *Brecht v. Abrahamson*, 507 U.S. 619, 622 (1993) (defining habeas standard for relief as requiring a showing of a "substantial and injurious effect or influence in determining the jury's verdict")

Changing Presumptions and Burden's of Proof

The standard of review is the standard the appellate court will use in reviewing the lower court's ruling, and except for cases where the appellate court uses "de novo" standard of review, the "standard of review" is not the same test that was used to make the ruling on the alleged error.

For example, if a trial judge made a ruling concerning the admission of evidence at the trial, the legal test for the admission of that evidence could be whether or not the evidence was relevant and whether or not the probative value of the evidence was substantially outweighed by the prejudicial value of the evidence[111].

---

[111] See Title 12 O.S. §§2401, 2402 and 2403

However, on appeal the "standard of review" on this type of issue will typically be an "abuse of discretion standard", which means the appellate court will not reverse the conviction unless the judge's decision was an "abuse of discretion" and the legal error survives the harmless error analysis.

The same issue will have different standards of review (or different presumptions and different burdens of proof) at various stages of the criminal justice system, and this is important to understand because when you are appealing a conviction, it is not enough to just argue the rule of law that applied at the trial court level. Your argument must also address the "standard of review" that is appropriate for the alleged legal error and you must generally also address the "harmless error" standard, assuming harmless error applies to that issue.

For example, if at trial a lawyer requested a self defense jury instruction, the lawyer may argue the issue of the jury instruction like this using the (**I.R.A.C method**) :

I.R.A.C-Trial - Requested Self Defense Jury Instruction

What is the **I**ssue?

Is the defendant entitled to have the jury instructed concerning the right to self defense?

What is the **R**ule of Law?

"As a general proposition a defendant is entitled to an instruction as to any recognized defense for which there exists evidence sufficient for a reasonable jury to find in his favor." *Mathews v. United States*, 485 U.S. 58, 63 (1988) Oklahoma law recognizes self defense as a defense as long as the force used was reasonable and the person was in fear of death or serious bodily injury[112].

Apply the Law to the Facts?

Self defense is a recognized defense, if a person used reasonable force and was in fear of death or serious bodily injury, and the defendant testified that he pointed the firearm because he was in fear of death or serious bodily injury. If the jury were to believe the defendant's testimony and believe the amount of force was reasonable, there is sufficient evidence to find that the defendant was acting in self defense.

---

[112] For the actual instruction see OUJI-CR-8-46

Conclusion

The defendant is entitled to have the jury in his trial instructed upon the law of self defense.

So let's say, using this example, that the judge overruled the request for a self defense jury instruction, the defendant was convicted and on direct appeal, and one of the propositions of error is the failure of the trial court to give the self defense instruction.

So on direct appeal the argument for this proposition of error is not just that the lower court's decision was legally wrong, meaning it was an "error" or meaning the defendant should have received a self defense instruction, the proposition must go further than that and explain why that the error meets the applicable "standard of review" which for our example we will say is an "abuse of discretion."

So in our example, the judge refuses to give a self defense instruction, the defendant is convicted, and the defendant appeals. On direct appeal at the Oklahoma Court of Criminal Appeals, this issue will be determined by an "abuse of discretion standard". (An abuse of discretion is any unreasonable or arbitrary action made without proper consideration of the relevant facts and law, also described as a clearly erroneous conclusion and judgment, clearly against the logic and effect of the facts. *Neloms v. State*, 2012 OK CR 7, ¶ 35, 274 P.3d 161, 170.)

So on direct appeal the issue is no longer a question of whether the defendant was "...entitled to an instruction as to any recognized defense for which there exists evidence sufficient for a reasonable jury to find in his favor"[113], the issue on appeal is whether or not the trial court judge abused the Court's discretion in refusing to give that instruction. Meaning the defendant would have to show <u>more than</u> "...there exists evidence sufficient for a reasonable jury to find in his favor", but that the trial judge's decision to deny the jury instruction was "unreasonable or arbitrary action made without proper consideration of the relevant facts and law, also described as a clearly erroneous conclusion and judgment, clearly against the logic and effect of the facts. (see *Neloms v. State*, 2012 OK CR 7, ¶ 35, 274 P.3d 161, 170).

---

[113] *Mathews v. United States*, 485 U.S. 58, 63 (1988)

On appeal there is a generally[114] a presumption that the trial court made the right decision and to overcome that presumption there is a higher burden. Because of the higher burden of proof (the "standard of review") it is entirely possible that the judges on the appellate court could believe that the judge's decision was not the correct decision, but it was not "an abuse of discretion" and deny the claim because the defendant could not meet the standard of review on appeal. The court could deny a proposition of error even though they personally would have made a different a decision at the trial court level.[115]

Even, when a defendant is able to meet the abuse of discretion standard, most appellate issues must be analyzed through the "harmless error" analysis, meaning not only should a defendant focus on proving there was a mistake at the district court level that meets the appropriate standard of review, they should also explain to the Court how that error harmed their case.

Let's take the same issue, the trial court not giving the self defense instruction and change it slightly where the trial attorney did not request the self defense instruction.

Failure to object is a waiver of all issues except for "plain error". Now the defendant has tougher presumptions and a more difficult burden of proof because the "plain error" standard of review is a more difficult standard.

Now with this same legal issue, whether or not the defendant was entitled to a self defense jury instruction, the analysis is more difficult using the "plain error" standard[116], which means the presumption against the defendant is stronger and the burden the defendant must prove is more difficult. Because the defendant's trial attorney did not object to the court excluding the self defense instruction (or failed to request the self defense instruction) now the

---

[114] There is not a higher burden with a *de novo* standard of review

[115] I know this may seem crazy that the appellate court could actually believe the trial judge made an error but still not reverse the conviction because it was not bad enough of a mistake, but this is how the system works.

[116] The "plain error standard" is a standard of review generally used when an attorney fails to object at trial.

appellate court will now find that the error is waived except for "plain error". Plain error is described as:

> ...this Court determines whether the appellant has shown an actual error, which is plain or obvious, and which affects his or her substantial rights. This Court will only correct plain error if the error seriously affects the fairness, integrity or public reputation of the judicial proceedings or otherwise represents a miscarriage of justice. Id. *Hogan v. State*, 2006 OK CR 19, ¶ 38, 139 P.3d 907, 923. See also *Jackson v. State*, 2016 OK CR 5, ¶ 4, 371 P.3d 1120, 1121; *Levering v. State*, 2013 OK CR 19, ¶ 6, 315 P.3d 392, 395.

(See *Fredrick v State*, 400 P.3d 786 (Okla.Crim. 2017))

So now because the trial attorney did not request a self defense instruction, on appeal the defendant must prove that the error was "plain or obvious" and that the error "seriously affects the fairness, integrity or public reputation of the judicial proceedings or otherwise represents a miscarriage of justice."

This is a tougher standard than it would have been if the trial attorney had objected. Remember, generally speaking, the later in the process an issue is raised, the more difficult the presumptions are to overcome and the higher the burden of proof or tougher "standard of review" will be applied; if an issue should have been raised at trial and was not raised until later in the process on appeal the "standard of review" will generally be tougher.

Often times when there is a failure to object by the trial counsel, the appellate attorney will raise the issue as "ineffective assistance of counsel". This doesn't necessarily solve the problem of the tougher "standard of review", because the presumptions and burden of proof associated with claims of ineffective assistance of counsel[117] are also tougher than the standard of review that would have applied if the trial counsel had not done or failed to do whatever it is that the appellate counsel is claiming is ineffective assistance of counsel.

---

[117] Often times state evidentiary issues are raised as ineffective assistance of counsel (IAC) because it raises the issue of whether the defendant's 6th Amendment constitutional right to effective assistance of counsel was violated and by raising an issue as IAC the issue is "federalized" and creates an issue that could potentially be successful in a federal habeas proceeding.

To prevail on an ineffective assistance of counsel claim, a defendant must show both that counsel's performance was deficient and that the deficient performance prejudiced his defense. In order to show ineffective assistance of counsel, a defendant must first show that the attorney's representation fell below "an objective standard of reasonable-ness." Second, a defendant must prove that the attorney's inadequate representation prejudiced the defendant. A defendant is prejudiced when "there is a reasonable probability that, but for counsel's unprofessional errors, the result of the proceeding would have been different." *Strickland v. Washington*, 466 U.S. 668, 687, 104 S. Ct. 2052, 80 L. Ed. 2d 674 (1984).

Once again there are strong presumptions that make these claims more difficult because reviewing courts "indulge a strong presumption that counsel's conduct" was constitutionally adequate and that "judicial scrutiny of counsel's performance must be highly deferential." With ineffective assistance of counsel claims there is a very difficult burden of persuasion or "standard of review".

The issue becomes even more difficult if the issue was not raised by both trial counsel and appellate counsel. In this situation, a defendant must argue ineffective assistance of appellate counsel and must prove that no reasonable appellate lawyer would have failed to raise an issue and that the defendant would have prevailed on the claim if it had been raised.

So let's say the defendant loses this issue on direct appeal, then the issue has been exhausted in the state court proceedings. *Res Judicata* means issues that were raised and decided on direct appeal are barred from further consideration on post conviction relief, basically the courts are saying we already told you no once don't ask again. (See *Paxton v. State*, 910 P.2d 1059). Keep this in mind a defendant cannot come back on state post conviction relief (Title 22 OS Section 1080) and re-urge the argument.[118] The defendant could

---

[118] Post-conviction review does not afford defendants opportunity to reassert claims in hopes that further argument alone may change the outcome in different proceedings. *Trice v State*, 912 P2d 349 (1996) and Defendants may not obtain review of issue raised previously by presenting it in a slightly different manner on post conviction relief. *Williamson v. State*, 852 P2d 167 (1993). "The Post-Conviction Procedure Act is not intended to provide a second appeal." *Richie v State*, 957 P.2d 1192 (1998)

raise this issue in Federal Habeas[119], but once again the presumption and the burden of proof becomes even tougher to overcome.

To overcome a ruling made by a state appellate court in a federal habeas proceeding, a defendant typically must establish that the ruling was "contrary to, or involved an unreasonable application of, clearly established Federal law, as determined by the Supreme Court of the United States" or that the decision was based upon an "unreasonable determination of the facts in light of the evidence presented in the State court proceeding." This is a tougher standard, not only does the decision have to be wrong, it must be contrary to clearly established Federal law, as determined by the United States Supreme Court or it must involve an unreasonable determination of the facts.

First, there is a presumption that the trial court made the right decision, and now that the state appellate court affirmed the decision, there is now another presumption that the state appellate court reached the right decision. As a defendant's case progresses through the criminal justice system, it becomes harder and harder to win the case because of the increasing burdens. I say generally because there are instances even in federal habeas where the courts will not defer to the lower court rulings, but every proposition of error will need to researched to determine the "standard of review" for each issue depending on the findings made by the lower courts to determine the proper standard of review.

So for every issue on direct appeal the following must be researched:
1. The correct rule of law to decide the legal issue at the trial court level.
2. The appropriate standard of review for that legal issue on direct appeal.

---

[119] Technically, this issue as explained could not be raised in federal court because it is based solely on state law, the issue would have had to been "federalized" (argued to involve a constitutional right). But this fact does not matter for our example.

3. Whether or not that legal issue requires a harmless error analysis.[120]

What is required to have a winning proposition of error on direct appeal? Generally, what is required is one of the following:

1. The trial court reached the wrong legal decision because the trial court failed to follow the rule of law[121] (or interpreted the rule of law incorrectly) and that error was sufficient to satisfy the harmless error analysis (if harmless error analysis is required).

2. The trial court reached the wrong legal decision because the trial court applied the wrong rule of law and that error was sufficient to satisfy the harmless error analysis (if harmless error analysis is required).

3. The trial court reached the wrong legal decision because the trial court based its decision on an unreasonable determination of facts and that error was sufficient to satisfy the harmless error analysis (if harmless error analysis is required).

4. Plain Error

5. Ineffective Assistance of Counsel

6. Newly Discovered Evidence

7. Prosecutorial Misconduct

General Principles when Planning an Appeal

1. After conviction, all of the burdens shift against the defendant, except for issues that involve de novo review. (Primarily, legal questions.)
2. If the trial court used the wrong legal standard, that is an abuse of discretion; but you still must survive the harmless error analysis.

---

[120] It is not be a bad idea to explain to an appellate court why the alleged error made a difference in every proposition, whether or not you believe that harmless error is required or not. An appeal is about process and you need to explain to the appellate court where the process broke down in a case and why that matters. If you cannot explain why it made a difference, you probably do not have anything to begin with.

[121] "Rule of Law" is not just statutory law, it also includes case law and constitutional law.

3. Legal decisions of the trial judge are easier to get reversed than factual findings, because with pure questions of law the more favorable standard of de novo review is used.
4. Not taking into account the quality of the various courts, <u>generally</u> speaking the higher a defendant goes into the criminal appellate process the more difficult it becomes to reverse the convictions because the presumptions and burdens of proof become more difficult for the defendant.
5. Generally speaking, the later in the process that an issue is raised, the more difficult it is to prevail on that issue.
6. All issues that do not involve a fundamental error generally must survive the "harmless error" analysis.

13. Fighting a Case After Direct Appeal

For most state court defendants, losing their direct appeal means they will have to continue the fight their convictions on their own. ("pro se[122]") States are not constitutionally required to provide attorneys for (non-death penalty) indigent defendants after direct appeal and most states do not do so[123]. To continue to fight a criminal conviction after losing a direct appeal, a defendant must have an issue that qualifies for either post-conviction relief under the appropriate state post conviction relief act (in Oklahoma state statute Title 22 O.S. § 1080) or they must fight the conviction using federal habeas (Title 28 United States Code § 2254)[124].

Pro se defendants fighting their cases after direct appeal must work hard to understand the appellate process and learn the law so they can file the best appeal possible[125]. **If a pro se defendant does manage to get a good issue into federal court on federal habeas, they stand a decent chance of having an attorney appointed to represent them.**

Pro se defendants should concentrate on using the state court post-conviction relief process to exhaust the claims they plan on asserting in federal habeas. Columbia Law School publishes a Jailhouse Lawyer's Manual to assist inmates and in particular pro se inmates. This manual can be downloaded from the internet at no charge or a paperback copy can be ordered online[126] for $30 for incarcerated persons. I highly recommend the Jailhouse Lawyer's Manual for pro se inmates fighting their convictions after direct appeal.

Oklahoma State Post-Conviction Relief Act

Oklahoma's post-conviction relief act can be found at Title 22 O.S. Section 1080 (2022) the act reads as follows:

---

[122] "for oneself" or "on one's own behalf".

[123] *Douglas v. California,* 372 U.S. 353 (1963)

[124] Federal Habeas for federal prisoners is governed by Title 28 United States Code § 2255

[125] If you know you will not have the money to hire a lawyer to fight your case after losing direct appeal, you may want to start reading and learning about the law before the court issues the opinion on your case.

[126] jlm.law.columbia.edu

Any person who has been convicted of, or sentenced for, a crime and who claims:

1. That the conviction or the sentence was in violation of the Constitution of the United States or the Constitution or laws of this state;

2. That the court was without jurisdiction to impose sentence;

3. That the sentence exceeds the maximum authorized by law;

4. That there exists evidence of material facts, not previously presented and heard, that requires vacation of the conviction or sentence in the interest of justice;

5. That the sentence has expired, the suspended sentence, probation, parole, or conditional release unlawfully revoked, or he or she is otherwise unlawfully held in custody or other restraint; or

6. That the conviction or sentence is otherwise subject to collateral attack upon any ground of alleged error heretofore available under any common law, statutory or other writ, motion, petition, proceeding or remedy, may institute a proceeding under the Post-Conviction Procedure Act in the court in which the judgment and sentence on conviction was imposed to secure the appropriate relief. Excluding a timely appeal, the Post-Conviction Procedure Act encompasses and replaces all common law and statutory methods of challenging a conviction or sentence including, but not limited to, writs of habeas corpus.

Understanding Oklahoma's Post-Conviction Relief Act

On November 1, 2022 Title 22 O.S. § 1080.1 went into effect establishing a one (1) year statute of limitations for filing of claims under the Oklahoma Post-Conviction Relief Act. Defendants must pay close attention to the statute of limitations.

State post-conviction is an important part of fighting a conviction after losing a direct appeal, because before a defendant can be granted relief through federal habeas, the claims must be exhausted in state court first. Exhaustion means the issue raised in federal habeas must have been raised at the state court level and the state court must have been given an opportunity to decide the issue.

Furthermore, federal court's will not grant habeas on issues of state law; the issue must involve federal law, not state law alone.

Ideally speaking, an attorney handling the direct appeal for a defendant would raise all of the issues that could be raised in both state and federal court in a manner that would allow a defendant to go directly to federal court on federal habeas if he or she had an issue that they could pursue on habeas. If all of the issues are raised on direct appeal are argued in a manner that "federalizes" the issues, state post conviction is not necessary and the issues are cleaner because it removes a level of complexity that is created by having to go through the state post-conviction relief process.

However, in my experience, many state appellate lawyers generally focus on winning the case on direct appeal and do not typically look towards a federal habeas. This adds layers of complexity because of doctrines of waiver and res judicata. Waiver means that post-conviction claims which could have been raised on direct appeals, but were not raised, are generally (in most jurisdictions) considered waived. (See *Walker v. State*, 933 P2d 327; *Ex parts Nelson*, 308 S.W. 3d 221, Tex.Crim.App. 2010, *Witherspoon v. State*, 969 So. 2d 289, Fla. 2007 and *State v. Brooks*, 960 S.W. 2d 479. Mo. bang 1997) *Res Judicata* means issues that were raised and decided on direct appeal are barred from further consideration on post conviction relief, basically the courts are saying we already told you no once don't ask again. (See *Paxton v. State*, 910 P.2d 1059.)

This may seem like a catch 22 and it is. If an issue could have been raised on direct appeal and was not, it is considered to have been waived[127] and if it was raised and denied then it is "res judicata" and it cannot be argued again. Under Oklahoma law and most other states, post conviction relief is reserved only for rare set of circumstances where a particular claim could not have been raised on direct appeal. (See *Brecheen v Reynolds*, 41 F.3d 1343 (10th Cir. 1994)).

Post-conviction review does not afford defendants opportunity to reassert claims in hopes that further argument alone may change the outcome in different proceedings (See *Trice v State*, 912 P2d 349

---

[127] There are issues such as ineffective assistance of appellate counsel and newly discovered evidence that avoid the waiver issue on post conviction, but these issues come with their own problems.

(1996)) and defendants may not obtain review of issue raised previously by presenting it in a slightly different manner on post conviction relief. (See *Williamson v. State*, 852 P2d 167 (1993)). "The Post-Conviction Procedure Act is not intended to provide a second appeal." (See *Richie v State*, 957 P.2d 1192 (1998))

So if after reviewing a case an issue is uncovered that should have been raised on direct appeal and that could serve as a basis for federal habeas relief, the issue must be raised in a way that will not be barred by waiver and that will federalize the issue. Remember though, because the issue was raised later on in the process, this will generally mean that the standard of review or the presumptions and burdens of proof will be more difficult.

This is why lawyers working on post-conviction relief cases look for issues such as ineffective assistance of appellate counsel, newly discovered evidence and newly discovered claims of governmental misconduct. If you can argue that appellate counsel was ineffective by not raising a particular issue, then that excuses waiver. If this seems complicated, it is, our criminal justice system favors finality, and the system is designed to make it very difficult to get a conviction reversed. It helps to think of the criminal justice system as a funnel: the defendant has the best chance at the beginning of the system, as the case proceeds through the system the chance for relief gets smaller and smaller.

Ideally speaking state post-conviction would not be part of a successful federal habeas claim, because all of the issues would have been raised within the direct appeal and therefore the issue would have been exhausted in state court and the defendant could go straight into federal habeas. But if the issues were not raised on direct appeal, this is generally a defendant's last opportunity to get an issue into the record before federal habeas, so it should be explored. I would never recommend abandoning a good issue for federal habeas simply because simply because going through the state post conviction relief process would create a tougher standard of review for that issue. If a defendant has a good issue it should be pursued no matter how difficult the standard of review to get the case reversed will be. It only takes one good issue to get a conviction reversed.

Federal Habeas Corpus

There are numerous cases that were affirmed through the Oklahoma state court process only to be reversed by the federal courts using the federal habeas statute; death penalty cases are some of the most likely types of state court cases to get reversed, in part because death penalty defendants are entitled to appellate lawyers at state expense past direct appeal. However, if you do manage to get a legitimate federal habeas issue into the federal district court, the federal judges are pretty good about appointing lawyers to represent indigent state court defendants.

But to have a chance at having your conviction reversed by a federal court, you have to have the right facts and issues in your case (something you have little to no control over) and you must follow the procedural rules and make sound legal arguments (something you do have control over).

Habeas corpus is guaranteed by the Constitution to federal prisoners whose arrest, trial, or actual sentence violated a federal statute, treaty, or the U.S. Constitution. Federal habeas is also available for state prisoners and is governed by 28 U.S.C. § 2254. Because the U.S. Constitution is the only federal law that governs state criminal procedures, state prisoners, are restricted in the claims they can pursue and must show a violation of the U.S. Constitution to win a habeas petition. State prisoners who are seeking relief in federal court under the habeas statute (28 U.S.C § 2254) must meet the requirements of the Anti-Terrorism and Effective Death Penalty Act ("AEDPA"), which limits federal courts' ability to grant habeas relief when reviewing claims from state prisoners.

The flow of a state prisoner challenging their case in federal court using the federal habeas process will be:

First- State Direct Appeal[128]
Second- State Post Conviction Appeal[129]
Third- Federal Habeas Claim in Federal District Court
Fourth-Appeal to the Federal Circuit Court the Denial of Federal Habeas Claim by the Federal District Court

---

[128] If you loose the direct appeal you can appeal the denial to the United States Supreme Court with a Petition for a Writ of Certiorari, but that is a real long shot.

[129] You must fully exhaust the state process including all available state appeals

Fifth-Appeal of Denial by the Federal Circuit to the United States Supreme Court

For a state prisoner seeking habeas relief, (28 U.S.C. § 2254[130]), to obtain federal habeas relief, a defendant must show that their rights were violated, that the violation was not harmless, and that the state court's ruling was either:

1. an unreasonable decision that was contrary to clearly established federal law or

2. involved unreasonable determination of the facts in light of the evidence presented in the state court proceeding.

This is a difficult standard to meet, this means that to get federal habeas relief, a state court defendant cannot just show the federal court that the state court was wrong (meaning that they made a legal error), a state court defendant must persuade the federal court that the state court's ruling was "unreasonable" or "contrary" to the Supreme Court's interpretation of federal law or involved unreasonable determination of the facts in light of the evidence presented in the State court proceeding. This is why it is important for state court criminal defense trial lawyers to know United States Supreme Court law, and to object when appropriate, and make a good record at trial. Whether or not a defendant is ultimately successful on federal habeas could depend on whether or not their trial attorney objected at trial and knew United States Supreme Court case law well enough to make a proper record.

How the federal court will apply the AEDPA standard of review will depend on how the state court handled a defendant's claims. If the state court adequately addressed an issue, then the federal court will apply the AEDPA highly deferential standard of review to the state court's decision-making process. However, if the state court failed to adequately address an issue, the federal court will apply a less deferential standard, meaning that the standard of review will be more favorable for the defendant. The federal court will look to see if the state court's decision was "unreasonable" or "contrary" to the Supreme Court's interpretation of the law or involved unreasonable

---

[130] §2254 applies to state prisoners seek federal relief while §2255 applies to federal prisoners seeking habeas relief.

determination of the facts in light of the evidence presented in the state court proceeding. In addition to demonstrating that the state court's decision-making process was incorrect, a defendant still needs to provide facts that show that the state court's ultimate determination was incorrect.

A pro se state court defendant, who is forced to represent themselves after the denial of their direct appeal, needs to read and understand 28 U.S.C. § 2254 before they file any state post conviction claim. The reason a pro se state court defendant needs to understand the requirements of § 2254 is understanding what is required to succeed in federal habeas will shape the arguments that are made in the state post conviction proceedings. The state court claims need to be in line with the requirements of 28 U.S.C. § 2254.

Fourth Amendment Claims (Search and Seizure Claims)

Generally, claims based on Fourth Amendment violations (unlawful search and seizure) are not allowed to be pursued in federal court because the federal courts do not have jurisdiction in habeas corpus actions, see *Stone v. Powell*, 428 U.S. 465 (1976).

The reasoning behind the *Stone* case is that the purpose of the Fourth Amendment's exclusionary rule, mainly the deterrence of future unlawful police conduct – would not be furthered by applying the rule on collateral review of cases in which full and fair consideration of the claim had already been given by the state courts. There are some exceptions to *Stone v. Powell*, but there are not many cases that will fit into those exceptions[131]. If you wish to pursue a federal habeas action based upon a Fourth Amendment claim, you will need to research the issue and *Stone v. Powell* and the cases that cite *Stone v. Powell* is a good place to start.

What is Required to Get Federal Relief

Habeas applicants who meet the procedural requirements of federal habeas are entitled to relief only when the conviction is contrary to clearly established federal law, or that involved an unreasonable application of clearly established federal law (was "based on an unreasonable determination of the facts in light of the evidence presented") and when they demonstrate actual prejudice (in

---

[131] Ineffective Assistance of Counsel *Kimmelman v. Morrison*, 477 U.S. 365 (1986), New constitutional Rule *Teague v Lane*, 489 U.S. 288 (1989)

other words survived the harmless error analysis). (See *Brecht v. Abrahamson*, 507 U.S. 619 (1993))

"Demonstrate actual prejudice" is a requirement that a defendant shows that it actually mattered in his or her particular case. Courts also refer to this as the "harmless error" analysis. For example, lets say that a defendant is seeking federal habeas for a conviction, and that at the trial the state introduced multiple eye witnesses, a video of the defendant committing the crime, DNA evidence, a note written by the defendant explaining how the defendant intended on committing the crime, and the murder weapon; in a case like that it probably did not make a difference in the outcome of the case that the police illegally obtained a confession. Why? Because it would not have made a difference. Even if the confession was excluded from the trial, the state still had overwhelming evidence of the defendant's guilt and the outcome would have been the same. Generally speaking, the stronger the state's case against a defendant, the more difficult it is to get the conviction reversed even if there was a legal error.

This means that a defendant may have had evidence introduced at their trial that was obtained in violation of their Constitutional rights, and that alone may not be enough to get the conviction reversed."The facts underlying the claim would be sufficient to establish by clear and convincing evidence that but for constitutional error, no reasonable fact finder would have found the applicant guilty of the underlying offense." (See 28 U.S.C. § 2254(e)(2))

A state court decision is "contrary to" U.S. Supreme Court precedent if the state court "applies a rule that contradicts the governing law set forth in [U.S. Supreme Court] cases" or if the state court "confronts a set of facts that are materially indistinguishable from a decision of the [U.S. Supreme] Court and nevertheless arrives at a result different from precedent." *Williams v. Taylor*, 529 U.S. 362, 406 (2000) As you can imagine there are many cases where there is no "materially indistinguishable" decisions from the United States Supreme Court.

A state court's decision involves an "unreasonable application of clearly established Federal law" when its application is objectively unreasonable. For example, an unreasonable application occurs when a state court correctly identifies the applicable legal principle, but unreasonably applies the legal principle to the facts. A federal court may grant relief when a state court has misapplied a "governing legal principle" to "a set of facts different from those of the case in which the principle was announced." *Lockyer v. Andrade*, 538 U.S. 63, 76 (2003)

Unreasonable is different than incorrect and a "...federal habeas court may not issue the writ simply because that court concludes in its independent judgment that the relevant state court decision applied clearly established federal law erroneously or incorrectly. Rather, that application must also be unreasonable." See *Prince v. Vincent*, 538 U.S. 634 (2003) (just because the appellate court found the lower court was incorrect, it was not objectively unreasonable given that other courts reached similar conclusions). This is an important point: if you are researching an issue and you find other courts that ruled similar to the court that denied your appeal, on the issue that you are planning your habeas appeal on, you are probably not on solid legal ground.

A federal court may also grant habeas relief based on a state court's "unreasonable determination of the facts in light of the evidence presented in the state court proceedings." (See 28 U.S.C. § 2254(d)(2)) In *Wiggins v. Smith*, the U.S. Supreme Court found that a state court had both unreasonably applied clearly established federal law and unreasonably determined facts in the state court proceedings. The claim in Wiggins was an ineffective assistance of counsel the U.S. Supreme Court held that even if the legal standard used was correct, the decision involved an unreasonable application of clearly established law by adding an additional requirement.

A federal court may only grant relief based on a state court's determination of facts if the state court's ruling "resulted in a decision that was based on an unreasonable determination of the facts in light of the evidence presented in the state court proceeding." 28 U.S.C. § 2254(d)(2) State court factual findings are presumed to be correct, 28 U.S.C. § 2254(e)(1) and you must have clear and convincing evidence to overcome the presumption. (See *Townsend v. Sain*, 372 U.S. 293 (1963); see also *Miller v. Fenton*, 474 U.S. 104 (1985); see also *Thompson v. Keohane*, 516 U.S. 99 (1995)). When the state court fails to resolve the factual issues or to provide for a full and fair hearing, the presumption of correctness does not apply. So a defendant who has a case where the state court did not make factual findings has a lower burden of proof as it relates to the factual determinations than a defendant in which the state court made a factual finding. This is another important point: often times state court district judges in Oklahoma will not take pro se post conviction proceedings seriously and as a result they will issue denials without evidentiary hearings or factual findings[132]. This is not necessarily a bad thing for a pro se defendant. I understand defendants find it frustrating that a judge does not take their your post conviction application seriously, however, that may benefit that defendant when they get the case into federal district court.

Developing a Strategy for Fighting Convictions

If a defendant has the resources, the best thing for them to do is to hire a lawyer that they trust to handle their direct appeal. A defendant can hire a lawyer to handle their direct appeal after a court appointed lawyer has been appointed on direct appeal as long as they have time to write the brief before it is due. If a defendant does not have the money to hire a lawyer and they lose their direct appeal then they will have to represent themselves in most cases. So how should a defendant go about preparing for the appeal?

First thing is you need to keep in mind is that you must start immediately, because there are time limitations on the Oklahoma Post-Conviction Relief Act (1 year) and with the AEDPA. (1 year from the time conviction becomes final, excluding time pursuing post-conviction relief. This means that once the Application for Post-Conviction Relief has been filed, not preparing to file.) A defendant needs to research the statute of limitations associated with both their state court post-conviction relief act and the AEDPA, make sure the understand the current[133] requirements of the law and make sure they plan accordingly.

Gathering Transcripts, Copies of Exhibits and Original Record

You have to have a copy of your transcripts and the Original Record (pleadings filed in the case) and any exhibits. Most

---

[132] In my experience I believe that most denials of state court post conviction applications are actually drafted by the prosecution.

[133] The law changes constantly, so do not presume the law referenced in this book is current. You must research the current law.

defendants do not have copies of their transcripts because the agencies representing indigent defendants on appeal do not like to pay for the copying of transcripts.[134] You can write your appellate attorney and ask them to send the transcript to you or to allow a friend or family member to copy the transcript. (I would keep a copy of this letter, it may be an issue later on.)

Defendants file motions in state district court all of the time asking for transcripts to be provided to the defendant at "state expense" after their direct appeal has been denied, judges routinely ignore and or deny these motions. <u>These transcripts have already transcribed and they are in the file of the defendants case</u>, so in the request for transcripts I would point that out. If you have a trial judge that wants to be fair, but is reluctant to order the court fund to pay for transcripts, it just might make a difference if the judge understands that the transcripts have already been transcribed and are just sitting in the file. It may also make a difference to a federal judge later on if it only costs the state a minimal amount of money, (only mailing), to provide the transcripts to an indigent defendant and the state court judge still refuses[135]. (This may be an equal protection argument, meaning it is legal problem for the state that indigent defendants do not have the same access to the criminal justice system as non-indigent defendants. This may also set up a Due Process of law argument.)

If the defendant's appellate lawyer returned their copy to the clerk's office then there are two copies of the transcripts in the file. If the appellate attorney returned their copy I would ask the court to order the clerks office to mail the defense copy of the transcripts to the defendant. If the appellate attorney had not returned the transcripts I would ask the attorney for the entire file. Either way, the

---

[134] If I were a defendant being represented on appeal by a court appointed attorney I would write a letter requesting a copy of the transcripts and original record <u>before</u> the brief was filed and I would ask friend or families to pay for copies. It is also a good idea to have friends or families scan copies of all the paperwork concerning the case. After the appeal is over OIDS will often times return the "trial file" to the lawyer who handled the trial. I would write OIDS and ask for my trial file after the direct appeal decision was issued. If you get the trial file ask a friend or family member to scan that file and to save the digital copy in multiple places.

[135] *Griffin v Illinois*, 351 U.S. 12 (1956) and *Britton v. United States*, 4040 U.S. 226 (1971)

defendant should be entitled to the copy of the transcripts that his lawyer used to do the direct appeal.

Sadly, many trial courts stonewall defendants, and in my opinion some courts do not want them to have copies of the transcripts because they do not want to deal with the inevitable post-conviction applications that will result from turning over the transcripts. But you have to have a copy of the transcripts.[136]

Remember appeals are about flaws in the process, if the trial court is corrupting the process by not seriously addressing the arguments of an indigent defendant or refusing to allow an indigent defendant access to trial transcripts that have already been prepared and just sitting in the court file, that is a flaw in the process that is fundamentally unfair. To challenge something a defendant believes is a flaw in the process, a defendant must first research the issue to see if it is a violation of a constitutional right, file a motion, and give a sufficient factual and legal basis for the request, and give them the opportunity to make the right.

It may also be possible to have the court clerk copy the transcript for a family member and mail it to a defendant. This will cost you, but it is cheaper (generally 25 cents a page) than buying a copy from the court reporter. Some court clerks will not allow you to copy the transcripts out of the file, but some will.

You can always purchase a copy of the transcripts from the court reporter. In the past my clients have been charged $1 a page[137], but you can negotiate with them and I have seen some court reporters cut people a deal. Most court reporters like selling copies of transcripts they have already been paid to transcribe, because all they have to do is print the transcripts.

In addition to the transcripts, the original record and copies of the exhibits, you will need the briefs filed in the direct appeal and the

---

[136] If I were a defendant that was denied a copy of my transcripts and I could not afford to buy a copy I would make a due process of law and equal protection argument based upon the trial court's refusal to allow my access to the transcripts that had been transcribed and are just sitting in the file. Such an argument would be started at the trial court level on post conviction and taken up to the Court of Criminal Appeals before taken to federal court. This may not get the conviction reversed, but it may cause a court to order the transcripts be given to an indigent defendant or even possibly excuse a waiver for not raising an issue.

[137] I have had court reporters charge me $1.50 per page

opinion of the Court of Criminal Appeals denying the direct appeal. If you can get it you will also want copies of the discovery (police reports, photographs and any digital media) in the case.

If I were a defendant who wanted to fight my conviction after direct appeal and I had to fight it on my own, I would ask my family to buy a copy of my transcripts and get copies of the pleadings in my district court and appellate file instead of asking them to "put money on my books". The average direct appeal takes at least a year, I would start trying to obtain a copy of my transcripts as soon as they had been transcribed and I would not wait for the direct appeal to be denied before I would start working on getting together a copy of my file. Especially, if I knew I would have to pursue post-conviction and federal habeas on my own, I would want to have my file together and I would already be learning the law just in case I lost the direct appeal.

If you cannot get your transcripts any other way and you ask the Court to give you your transcripts and the Court denies that request, that is an appealable order, even if you lose you have to make a record, if you do not make a record you very well may waiving an issue you can never get back. There are lots of problems in Oklahoma and other states when it comes to indigent defendants and access to the court files, the evidence in their cases (police reports etc), and transcripts. Problem areas of the law present opportunities for defendants who are appealing their convictions, remember appeals are about process, problems in the process create an opportunity for reversals. If a pro se defendant in prison cannot get copies of the transcripts, they can get some citations to facts from the appeal briefs filed in the case. A defendant could also include the lack of access to transcripts as a separate appeal issue (denial of due process) in a post-conviction and or habeas petition and brief if they explained and documented[138] the efforts they took to obtain the transcripts.

---

[138] I would start by raising the lack of access to transcripts issue at the trial court level and then attaching copies of the motions and or letters trying to get transcripts as exhibits to the state post conviction proceedings at the district court level. You have to begin the issue at the state court district court level and carry that issue all the way through to federal court.

Identify All Potential Issues

After you gather everything you want to start looking for issues. By this point you may already know the issues you want to raise, that is fine, but you still need to go through the process of looking for more issues. Start with making a list of everything that could possibly be an issue.

I would start by making a list of everything that was objected to at trial or before trial in the form of written objections. Objections the defense won will generally not serve as a basis for an appeal, but make sure you include every issue the defense lost in the potential issue list. Then go through and add to the list every issue that was not objected to, for example the failure of the lawyer to object to prejudicial evidence, newly discovered evidence, jury instructions, request lesser included offenses, any plea offer issues, any issues involving bad legal advice, failure to secure expert witnesses, failure to investigate the case, refusal to present favorable evidence, prosecutorial misconduct, failure to present evidence, and anything else you can think of.

Once I was satisfied that I had a complete list of everything that could possibly be an issue I would start my legal research. While performing legal research you may come across other potential issues, if you do add them to the list.

Research the Law to the Narrow the issues

I do not know what your law library may look like or what resources they should have. However, if you have access to the annotated statutes of your jurisdiction, I would go to the post-conviction relief statute in your jurisdiction and read the cases summarized after that statute. (The Oklahoma Statutes Annotated, these are small green books, the post-conviction relief statute is found at title 22 O.S. Section 1080.) This will help you understand what qualifies post-conviction in your jurisdiction. If you have the federal statutes annotated you can do the same thing for the federal habeas statute.

You need to read the rules of the appellate court that will be deciding your post-conviction claim, of the federal courts you will be filing your claim in and the Federal Rules of Appellate Procedure.

You need to read, read, read. Read the cases, take notes, think about what the Court is saying, think about the reasoning the court uses; when reading the opinions identify the **I**ssue, think about the **R**ule the court uses for that issue, notice the **A**pplication of the rule to the facts of the case and pay attention to the **C**onclusion the court reaches. The more cases you read the more you will start to understand the issues.

Read the cases cited in the appellate briefs in your case, read the cases cited in the opinion denying your direct appeal. Read the cases those cases cite and keep reading until you are confident that you have found the relevant law, understand the law and can articulate it.

While you research your issues you need to pay particular attention not only the rule of law that you believed was involved in your case, but the "standard of review" the appellate courts will use depending on which stage of the appellate process you are at. As described above these "standards of reviews", or presumptions and burdens as I like to call them, change not only at different stages of the appellate process, but can change for a particular issue depending on when it was raised and how the appellate court ruled. This is the heart of the appeal, this is the law you must first find, then understand and finally be able to correctly articulate, and argue to the appellate court. You must be able to do this if you want to have any chance of winning your appeal.

The goal of this step is to take the complete list of everything that could be an issue and go through the issues one by one and eliminate the issues that do not really work legally, keep narrowing the issues eliminating the ones that do not work or that are very unlikely to succeed until you have a set of your best issues.

Writing your Brief

In Oklahoma[139] for post-conviction and federal habeas, there are forms that you can complete and submit, you should use these forms. However, you should also file a brief in support of the Post Conviction or Habeas Petition (reference in the post conviction or habeas pleadings that you are filing a brief in support contemporaneously.) Generally, the Courts are more forgiving with pro se defendants, but I would do my best to make my brief in support look as much like the briefs from my attorney and the state in

---

[139] Most if not all state courts will have post conviction forms.

my direct appeal, try to make your brief so good the judges will wander if you had legal assistance in writing the brief.
1. Raise each issue as a separate proposition. Do not combine multiple issues into a single proposition of error.
2. For each proposition, make sure you include citations to the transcript or record to support your factual assertions about what occurred in your case; if you have the transcripts, failure to cite to the facts to provide a factual basis could waive the issue. If I was indigent and had been denied my transcripts, I would state this in the brief and attach evidence showing I requested transcripts and was denied, and then I would do my best to summarize the evidence without the citation to transcripts. Remember make a record and if you don't raise it you waive it, if the state court denied my access to transcripts that I needed to pursue my appeal, I would put it in the brief and would make that a separate proposition of its own arguing I was denied the right to equal protection, due process of law (in separate propositions of error) by the court's denial of access to the transcripts, then every place I needed to point to the transcripts, I would point instead to those propositions of error. On appeal sometimes you are talking to the next group of judges more than you are talking to the current group of judges.
3. For each proposition of error explain the rule of law you are claiming was violated and give at least one case to support your explanation of the law (do you best to make sure the law you cite is current and good law), for each proposition give the "standard of review" and cite to at least one case that says that is the appropriate "standard of review".
4. Include the case citations for the law you cite.
5. Apply the facts of your case to the law and explain to the Court why the facts in your case warrant a finding of error and why they meet the appropriate "standard of review". Each rule of law will have multiple elements and often times those elements have their own rules or definitions. Take your time address each element of the rule of law and argue how that element has been prove in your case.
6. Address the issue of harmless error. Explain why this error mattered to your case. This will require you to give a general

summary of the evidence presented at the trial so that you can explain why the alleged legal error mattered. If you are being whinny it will be obvious when you try and argue harmless error. A defendant is entitled to a fair trial, not a perfect one. Don't be whinny. Use your time to talks about things that mattered, not things that did not.
7. Proofread the brief multiple times. Once you are done with the brief, put it away for a couple of days and go back to it with a fresh set of eyes. Keep reading and polishing the brief until it is as good as you can get it.
8. File the post-conviction and habeas forms and the accompanying brief.

Looking for an Appellate Lawyer

The best way for you to find a lawyer to help you on your appeal is to have a friend or a family member contact the lawyer for you. If a friend or family member contacts a lawyer for you give them some basic information to give to the lawyer. I would suggest they know your DOC or BOP number, your case number, and the county or jurisdiction (the court[140]) you were convicted out of, the crimes you were convicted of, whether or not the conviction was a result of a plea or a trial, whether or not there was a direct appeal and/or whether or not a post-conviction has been filed if the direct appeal was denied. If you don't have help on the outside, and you write lawyers asking for help I suggest you put all of this information in the letter.

When writing an attorney, until and unless they ask, DO NOT send them items that you want returned, DO NOT send them briefs or long rambling letters about the law. The longer the letter the less likely you are to have it read by the lawyer, so I would recommend you get to the point quickly. Print legibly and make sure your letter is not a struggle to read.

Most lawyers cannot afford to represent you for free. Do not be surprised if you have difficulty finding a private lawyer to represent you for free. Appeals take a lot of work, the majority of criminal

---

[140] The court will be listed at the top of any of the pleadings of your case. For example "In the District Court of Tulsa County State of Oklahoma" or "In the Northern District of Oklahoma".

lawyers do not understand how to do appeals and most lawyers cannot afford to represent people free of charge. When you ask a lawyer to represent you for free you are asking that lawyer to give you thousands of dollars of their time and you are one of many people that will ask a lawyer to give away their services that year.

A lawyer cannot take a criminal case on a contingency[141] fee basis, this violates the rules of ethics. So offers to pay the lawyer out of funds you expect to receive from suing over your wrongful conviction and offering "movie and book rights" are not going to be helpful. Not to mention it's a rare case that a defendant has a viable claim for wrongful conviction. Wrongful conviction lawsuits are very difficult cases to win and the chances of selling the story for any money is even less likely than winning a lawsuit over the conviction. Do not try to hustle a lawyer into taking your appeal, the problem with hustling a lawyer to represent you on appeal, is that any lawyer dumb enough to fall for the hustle is probably too dumb to get your conviction reversed.

If you are an indigent state court defendant and cannot find a lawyer to represent you, I would focus on getting the best viable issues I could get into federal court on habeas. If you can get a good viable issue into federal court, you have a decent chance of having an attorney appointed by the federal judge handling your case.

---

[141] Contingent upon the outcome of the case.

14. Additional Appellate Resources

1. **A Jailhouse Lawyer's Manual** by Columbia University Law School. This manual can be found for free online at jlm.law.columbia.edu. This is a great resource for defendants fighting their conviction on their own. A Jailhouse Lawyer's Manual was first published in 1978 to help prisoners represent themselves in court. The late Supreme Court Justice Thurgood Marshall wrote the forward to the JLM which is copied below:

> A Jailhouse Lawyer's Manual is an important and impressive work. Although it is well-established that prisoners have a constitutional right to affirmative governmental assistance in the preparation and filing of legal papers, see *Bounds v. Smith*, 430 U.S. 817 (1976), state and federal prisoners often still lack the necessary information and resources to obtain effective and adequate judicial review. This manual will help alleviate that problem. Written in a clear, readable fashion, the manual provides an easy, step-by-step guide to assist prisoners in understanding and maneuvering their way through an increasingly complex legal system. By making difficult and sensitive legal issues accessible to the lay person, the manual helps to empower prisoners to exercise a right we, as a society, hold dear-the right to speak for oneself. I commend Columbia's law students for publishing so comprehensive and insightful a manual. A Jailhouse Lawyer's Manual should be read by everyone involved m, or concerned about, prisoners' rights.   Justice Thurgood Marshall February, 1992

2. **Georgetown Law Review Annual Review of Criminal Procedure** is a comprehensive survey of all criminal procedure in the federal courts. The ARCP is a single issue per year edition that provides readers with objective, concise and accurate overview of criminal procedure and recent case-law decisions in the United States Supreme Court and each of the 12 Federal Circuit Courts. This is a great resource, but they are difficult to order from, so you may want outside help to get this. From the Georgetown Law website-

> **To place a new inmate subscription order please contact Customer Service via email for the <u>discount inmate order form</u>.** (lawcriminalprocedure@georgetown.edu) Please know

our online order form does not support the discount rate for inmates. The current rate for inmates purchases is $25, which includes shipping and handling fees, if we ship directly to the inmate. We are required to collect tax if shipping to customers located in DC, MD, NY, TN, and VA. For tax rates please see the PDF order form. The completed form can be mailed or faxed to the address below for payment by check, money order or credit card. At this time we cannot accept orders with credit card via telephone or email.

Office of Journal Administration
Georgetown University Law Center
PO Box 382
Congers, NY 10920

Please make checks and money orders payable to: Georgetown Law Journals

All discount inmate order sales are final, refunds are not available.

3. **Tenth Circuit Court of Appeals Practitioner's Guide-** This guide is a pdf on the Tenth Circuit's website[142], it is over 100 pages and explains in detail the procedure for appellate process in the Tenth Circuit (the federal circuit for Oklahoma.)

"The 10th Circuit Practitioner's Guide is a tool designed to help practitioners understand court rules and procedures, and also includes information about the structure of the court, the judges of the 10th Circuit and other guidance regarding filing appeals and original proceedings."[143]

4. **Tenth Circuit Court of Appeals Pro Se Filer FAQ** -This is another free resource available on the Tenth Circuit's website under the forms tab and gives answers to frequently asked questions for pro se filers.

5. **Uniform Jury Instructions-**Uniform jury instructions can be found on OSCN.net or perhaps in the prison law library. They are called OUJIs for Oklahoma Uniform Jury Instructions. Uniform jury instructions are great resources for pro se defendants because they are written to explain the law to people without legal education so

---

[142] can be found under forms section of the website

[143] Copied From the Tenth Circuit Website

they explain the law in simple terms that are easy to understand. Additionally, the committee comments often times contain explanations of the law with citations to both statutes and cases.

6. **OIDS Unpublished Opinions Website-**The Oklahoma Indigent Defense System has a website of unpublished [144]Oklahoma Court of Criminal Appeals decisions that are organized by subjects matter. For example "Abuse of Discretion", "Due Process", "Ineffective Assistance of Counsel", "Prosecutor Misconduct" and "Statutory Construction" to name a few. This is a great resource for legal research to find published opinions. What is so helpful is that the cases are organized by subject matter. The website can be found through a simple google search of "OIDS Unpublished Opinions". The OIDS website also has a page that of "Monthly Unpublished Opinions Issued Where Relief was Granted", this is a great page because it list the unpublished opinions from the Oklahoma Court of Criminal Appeals where relief was granted.

7. **Pro Se Guidebook For Petitions For Writs of Habeas Corpus Governed by 28 U.S.C. § 2254-** The United States District Court for the District of Minnesota has on its website a this guide. This guide provides a lot of information that would be useful to any pro se habeas litigant. As of this writing the guide book is located at www.mnd.uscourts.gov/sites/mnd/files/2254-PrisonerGuidebook.pdf.

---

[144] Read Oklahoma Court of Criminal Appeals Rule 3.5 C(3) if you cite an unpublished opinion in a brief.

15. Faith

I was raised in the church and was devoted to my faith as a child, as I grew up I walked away from God. By the time I became a lawyer I had turned my back on my faith and I spent 20 years reading every self-help book that I thought was worth reading. It wasn't until I started reading the Bible again, that I found what I had been looking for all those years. I was filled with so much hate, so much anger and so much pain. I had the answer as a child and left it behind thinking I would find the truth in the world. My story is not uncommon, I think many people walk away from God and get lost in the world, I am just grateful for God's mercy that lead me back to Him. Faith is personal and each individual has to make their own decision, but I wanted to take this opportunity to share some of my thoughts about faith with the readers of this book.

> Seek ye the LORD while he may be found, call ye upon him while he is near: let the wicked forsake his way, and the unrighteous man his thoughts: and let him return unto the LORD, and he will have mercy upon him; and to our God, for he will abundantly pardon.
>
> Isaiah 55:6-7 KJV

God Uses Broken People

God uses broken people. Mosses was a murderer[145], King David had a man killed so he could hide the adultery he had committed with the man's wife;[146] the Apostle Peter cut a man's ear off[147] and the Apostle Paul[148] persecuted Christians; Moses, David, Peter and Paul were all sinners that were used mightily by God.

---

[145] Exodus 2:11-12

[146] 2 Samuel 11

[147] John 18:10-11

[148] Acts 8:1 and Philippians 3:6

One of my favorite parables is the parable of the Pharisee and the publican[149] in the 18th chapter of Luke:

> Two men went up into the temple to pray; the one a Pharisee, and the other a publican. The Pharisee stood and prayed thus with himself, God, I thank thee, that I am not as other men are, extortioners, unjust, adulterers, or even as this publican. I fast twice in the week, I give tithes of all that I possess. And the publican, standing afar off, would not lift up so much as his eyes unto heaven, but smote upon his breast, saying, God be merciful to me a sinner. I tell you, this man went down to his house justified rather than the other: for every one that exalteth himself shall be abased; and he that humbleth himself shall be exalted.
>
> Luke 18:10-14 KJV

It is like an AA or an NA meeting, when someone stands up to speak, the first thing they do is introduce themselves and admit that they are an alcoholic or an addict. A person cannot begin to fix a problem until they admit that they have a problem, and a person cannot repent of their sins until they admit that they are a sinner.

In the parable of the Pharisee and the publican, the publican knows he is a sinner and freely admits that he is a sinner, he will not look up to heaven and is asking God to have mercy on him. The Pharisee does not know he is a sinner. The publican is comparing himself to the standards that God has set out for him and that is why he is ashamed because he knows how broken he is and he needs God's mercy. The Pharisee is comparing himself to the publican and thanking God that he is not like the publican. The publican is measuring himself against God's standards and the Pharisee is measuring himself by his own.

We can always feel good about ourselves if we compare ourselves to our fellow man, but it is when we compare ourselves to God's standards that we realize just how broken we are. There are a lot of modern day Pharisees in and around the criminal justice system, that is what the "good guy vs. bad guy" thing is all about.

---

[149] Publicans were tax collectors for the Roman Empire, they were outcast among the Jewish people because they betrayed their own people, were know for cheating people and many were rich. See the story of Zaccheus in Luke 19:1-10.

When you call someone a "bad guy" that is a comparison and what you are actually saying is "I am good and he is bad". The Pharisee looked at the publican and thought that the publican was a bad guy, and he was right, what he was wrong about is the Pharisee thought that he himself was a good guy, because he was measuring himself according to the standards of man and not the standards of God.

The publican knew that he had a problem, the publican's problem was the sin nature of man. The Pharisee went away unjustified because he refused to admit he had a sinful nature and call upon God for his mercy. The Apostle Paul understood that he was sinful, "O wretched man that I am! who shall deliver me from the body of this death?" (Romans 7:24 KJV) The Apostle Peter knew that he was sinful, "When Simon Peter saw it, he fell down at Jesus' knees, saying, Depart from me; for I am a sinful man, O Lord." (Luke 5:8 KJV). It is because of the sin nature of man that "The heart is deceitful above all things, and desperately wicked: who can know it?" (Jeremiah 17:9 KJV)

Famous theologian C.S. Lewis said:

> A world of nice people, content in their own niceness, looking no further, turned away from God, would be just as desperately in need of salvation as a miserable world-and might be even more difficult to save.

The quote from C.S. Lewis, above described the Pharisee who was comparing himself to the standards of man and he liked what he saw and was "content in" his "own niceness." But the publican, the Apostle Paul, and the Apostle Peter compared themselves to the standards of God and knew they were broken, sinful, and shameful and as a result they knew they had a problem and they needed God's mercy and grace. You cannot receive God's mercy until you are willing to admit you need it and are willing to ask God for it.

In the Sermon on the Mount[150], Jesus gave us a description of the character of a true Christian in the "Beatitudes". In Matthew 5:3 Jesus said, "Blessed are the poor in spirit: for their's is the kingdom of heaven." (Matthew 5:3 KJV) The publican was "poor in spirit"; "And the publican, standing afar off, would not lift up so much as his

---

[150] Matthew Chapter 5 through 7

eyes unto heaven, but smote upon his breast, saying, God be merciful to me a sinner." (Luke 18:13 KJV) The Apostle Paul was "poor in spirit" as reflected by what he wrote in Romans 7, "O wretched man that I am! who shall deliver me from the body of this death?" (Romans 7:24 KJV). The Apostle Peter was "poor in spirt"; "When Simon Peter saw it, he fell down at Jesus' knees, saying, Depart from me; for I am a sinful man, O Lord." (Luke 5:8 KJV).

In the second "Beatitude" Jesus said, "Blessed are they that mourn: for they shall be comforted."(Matthew 5:4 KJV) What are they mourning about? The same thing the publican, the Apostle Paul, and the Apostle Peter were mourning about, their sinful nature and the sinful nature of the world.

In the third "Beatitude" Jesus said, "Blessed are the meek: for they shall inherit the earth."(Matthew 5:5 KJV) Why is the character of the true Christian "meek"? Because they know that they are a "sinner", a "wretched man", and "a sinful man".

In the fourth "Beatitude" Jesus said, "Blessed are they which do hunger and thirst after righteousness: for they shall be filled." (Matthew 5:6 KJV) Why is the true Christian hungering and thirsting after the righteousness of God? Because they are "poor in spirit" and they know that they cannot have any righteousness of their own. "But we are all as an unclean thing, and all our righteousnesses are as filthy rags..." (Isaiah 64:6 KJV).

So many people feel like Paul ("O wretched man that I am!...") or Peter ("Depart from me; for I am a sinful man, O Lord...") and are discouraged feeling like there is no hope for them. That is not true, they are the "poor in spirit" and these are exactly the type of people that God uses when they are willing to surrender their lives to him. "Come unto me, all ye that labour and are heavy laden, and I will give you rest. Take my yoke upon you, and learn of me; for I am meek and lowly in heart: and ye shall find rest unto your souls. For my yoke is easy, and my burden is light." (Matthew 11:28-30 KJV)

Faith Is About a Relationship With God

The goal is not to use Jesus to get what you want and need, what you need is Jesus; the goal is to change your heart so that you realize your biggest need is a relationship with God, the goal is to draw our hearts close to Christ, so you can have a relationship with Him. Many think of faith as rules they must follow to be worthy of God, that is what the Pharisee thought in the parable of the Pharisee and the publican, "...God, I thank thee, that I am not as other men are, extortioners, unjust, adulterers, or even as this publican. I fast twice in the week, I give tithes of all that I possess." The Pharisee was focused on himself, he was proud that he followed the rules[151], and yet he went away unjustified. Faith is about a relationship with God, not rules.

In the 7th chapter of Matthew, near the end of the Sermon on the Mount, Jesus said "Many will say to me in that day, Lord, Lord, have we not prophesied in thy name? and in thy name have cast out devils? and in thy name done many wonderful works? And then will I profess unto them, I never knew you: depart from me, ye that work iniquity." (Matthew 7:22-23 KJV) When Jesus said "...I never knew you: depart from me, ye that work iniquity" isn't he is saying "we never had a relationship?" Jesus said the same thing in the parable of the ten virgins in Matthew 25, "But he answered and said, Verily I say unto you, I know you not." (Matthew 25:12 KJV)

The greatest commandment is to love God with all our heart, soul and mind, Jesus tells us this in Matthew 22. "Jesus said unto him, Thou shalt love the Lord thy God with all thy heart, and with all thy soul, and with all thy mind. This is the first and great commandment." (Matthew 22:37-38 KJV) It is your heart that Christ wants, this is one of the themes of the Sermon on the Mount. Jesus also addressed this issue when he said "This people draweth nigh unto me with their mouth, and honoureth me with their lips; But their heart is far from me." (Matthew 15:8 KJV)

Sin separates us from God and stops us from having a relationship with him, "but your iniquities have separated between you and your God, and your sins have hid his face from you, that he will not hear."[152] (Isaiah 59:2 KJV) We cannot maintain a relationship with God if we continue to sin, we turn from sin not

---

[151] "Christ is become of no effect unto you, whosoever of you are justified by the law; ye are fallen from grace." Galatians 5:4 KJV

[152] "But unto the wicked God saith, What hast thou to do to declare my statutes, or that thou shouldest take my covenant in thy mouth?" Psalm 50:16 KJV

because following the rules makes us righteous[153], we turn from sin because He is righteous and maintaining our relationship with God is the most important thing in our lives. "If ye love me, keep my commandments." (John 14:15 KJV) The Apostle John talks about "walking in the light" and having "fellowship" with God, "If we say that we have fellowship with him, and walk in darkness, we lie, and do not the truth: but if we walk in the light, as he is in the light, we have fellowship one with another, and the blood of Jesus Christ his Son cleanseth us from all sin." (1 John 1:6-7 KJV)

When the Angel of the Lord appeared to Joseph in a dream to tell Joseph "...fear not to take unto thee Mary thy wife: for that which is conceived in her is of the Holy Ghost." (Matthew 1:20 KJV) The Angel told Jospeh "And she shall bring forth a son, and thou shalt call his name JESUS: for he shall save his people from their sins." (Matthew 1:21 KJV) Jesus was sent to us to save us from our sin, because our sin separates us from God. As the Apostle John put it "And ye know that he was manifested to take away our sins; and in him is no sin." (1 John 3:5 KJV)

Paul talks about it in the 5th chapter of Galatians when he said "For the flesh lusteth against the Spirit, and the Spirit against the flesh: and these are contrary the one to the other: so that ye cannot do the things that ye would." (Galatians 5:17 KJV). Peter talks about it "Dearly beloved, I beseech you as strangers and pilgrims, abstain from fleshly lusts, which war against the soul;" (1 Peter 2:11 KJV). And James[154], wrote about it in the 4th chapter of James:

> From whence come wars and fightings among you? come they not hence, even of your lusts that war in your members? Ye lust, and have not: ye kill, and desire to have, and cannot obtain: ye fight and war, yet ye have not, because ye ask not. Ye ask, and receive not, because ye ask amiss, that ye may consume it upon your lusts. Ye adulterers and adulteresses, know ye not that the friendship of the world is enmity with

---

[153] We can have no true righteousness of our own that is why we need God's righteousness. That is why we hunger and thirst after God's righteousness. See Matthew 5:6

[154] Jesus's brother (technically half-brother) not the Apostle James who was martyred by King Herod Agrippa in Acts 12

God? whosoever therefore will be a friend of the world is the enemy of God.

James 4:1-4 KJV

When we repent of our sins and accept Christ as our savior we are forgiven of our sins and made right with God, we are justified in the sight of God[155]; but we are also given the Spirit of God and we begin a process of sanctification by which we are changed from what we were, unto what God would have us to be. "Beloved, now are we the sons of God, and it doth not yet appear what we shall be: but we know that, when he shall appear, we shall be like him; for we shall see him as he is. And every man that hath this hope in him purifieth himself, even as he is pure. Whosoever abideth in him sinneth not: whosoever sinneth hath not seen him, neither known him." (1 John 3:2-3, 6 KJV)

In Second Peter 1, Peter describes this when he says "...that by these ye might be partakers of the divine nature, having escaped the corruption that is in the world through lust." (2 Peter 1:4 KJV) "Partakers of the Divine nature" means that we share in the Divine (of God) nature "having escaped the corruption that is in the world through lust."

All the corruption that is in this world comes into the world through lust. The world (and people in the world) are out of control and cannot control their lust. Whether it is food, sex, drugs, alcohol, fighting, jealousy, greed, or anger; people that "walk in the flesh" are unable to control themselves. If you think about the criminal justice system through its laws, arrests, convictions, punishment, "education", and imprisonment it is trying to replicate the fruits of the Spirit that Paul describes in Galatians 5:

> But the fruit of the Spirit is love, joy, peace, longsuffering, gentleness, goodness, faith, meekness, temperance: against such there is no law. And they that are Christ's have crucified the flesh with the affections and lusts.

---

[155] "Therefore being justified by faith, we have peace with God through our Lord Jesus Christ: by whom also we have access by faith into this grace wherein we stand, and rejoice in hope of the glory of God." Romans 5:1-2 KJV

Galatians 5:22-24 KJV

God is long-suffering, but He has his limits. "He, that being often reproved hardeneth his neck, Shall suddenly be destroyed, and that without remedy." (Proverbs 29:1 KJV) When people have rejected God and God is done with them, the Bible says He turns them over to their lust: "But my people would not hearken to my voice; And Israel would none of me. So I gave them up unto their own hearts' lust: And they walked in their own counsels." (Psalm 81:11-12 KJV) See also "Wherefore God also gave them up to uncleanness through the lusts of their own hearts, to dishonour their own bodies between themselves:" (Romans 1:24 KJV)

How many people do you know that were destroyed by their own lust? Have you ever known someone to drink themselves to death, abuse drugs until it killed them, eat themselves to death, or get themselves killed because of their greed? It could be any of the lusts of the flesh that lead to their destruction.

The criminal justice system is a physical solution for a spiritual problem; the real problem is that this world and those in the world need Jesus Christ, because he is the only cure for their sinful nature.

> Now the works of the flesh are manifest, which are these; Adultery, fornication, uncleanness, lasciviousness, idolatry, witchcraft, hatred, variance, emulations, wrath, strife, seditions, heresies, envyings, murders, drunkenness, revellings, and such like: of the which I tell you before, as I have also told you in time past, that they which do such things shall not inherit the kingdom of God.

Galatians 5:19-21 KJV

Over the years I have spoken to thousands of people facing criminal charges and I can tell you that many of them hate what they did, they hate that they keep doing it, and many have tried to stop and cannot. It reminds me of what Paul wrote in Romans 7:24 "O wretched man that I am! who shall deliver me from the body of this death?" Romans 7:24 KJV

In Galatians 5 Paul talks about how the Spirit and the flesh war against each other and if we walk after the Spirit we shall not fulfill the lust of the flesh.

> This I say then, Walk in the Spirit, and ye shall not fulfil the lust of the flesh. For the flesh lusteth against the Spirit, and the Spirit against the flesh: and these are contrary the one to the other: so that ye cannot do the things that ye would. ...And they that are Christ's have crucified the flesh with the affections and lusts.

Galatians 5:16-17, and 24 KJV

After accepting Christ we can be "partakers of the Divine nature" of God and we keep His commandments so that we can "walk in the light as he is in the light". We keep His commandments so that we can maintain our relationship with Him, as a Christian grows in their spiritual maturity they are able to maintain unbroken fellowship with God for longer and longer periods of time.

Some people act like God is a genie in a lamp and if you rub the lamp the right way, you can have all the things of this world that you want. "For the time will come when they will not endure sound doctrine; but after their own lusts shall they heap to themselves teachers, having itching ears; and they shall turn away their ears from the truth, and shall be turned unto fables." (2 Timothy 4:3-4 KJV) The bible is clear, "No man can serve two masters: for either he will hate the one, and love the other; or else he will hold to the one, and despise the other. Ye cannot serve God and mammon." (Matthew 6:24 KJV) In the Sermon on the Mount Christ said "for where your treasure is, there will your heart be also." (Matthew 6:21 KJV)

Christ alone is worth everything, to the man or woman of faith. In the 13th chapter of Matthew, Jesus gives us the treasure of the parable in the field:

> Again, the kingdom of heaven is like unto treasure hid in a field; the which when a man hath found, he hideth, and for joy thereof goeth and selleth all that he hath, and buyeth that field.

Matthew 13:44 KJV

Faith Humility Connection

There is a faith-humility connection that appears over and over again in the Bible. Other than the examples of Peter and Paul discussed above, other great examples of the faith humility connection in the Gospels, are in the 15th chapter of Matthew after a woman asked Jesus to free her daughter from a devil, Matthew 15:21-28, and when a centurion asked Jesus to heal his servant, Matthew 8:5-13.

All throughout the Bible it talks about how God hates pride, I suspect that is because pride being the opposite of humility, interferes with our ability to have faith. "But without faith it is impossible to please him: for he that cometh to God must believe that he is, and that he is a rewarder of them that diligently seek him." (Hebrews 11:6 KJV)

The Bible warns us over and over again about pride; "Pride goeth before destruction, And an haughty spirit before a fall." (Proverbs 16:18 KJV), "But he giveth more grace. Wherefore he saith, God resisteth the proud, but giveth grace unto the humble." (James 4:6 KJV), "For all that is in the world, the lust of the flesh, and the lust of the eyes, and the pride of life, is not of the Father, but is of the world." (1 John 2:16 KJV). As Christians, pride is our enemy and we must guard against it as we pursue the opposite of pride, which is humility.

Remember what Jesus said in the Parable of the Pharisee and the Publican, "I tell you, this man went down to his house justified rather than the other: for every one that exalteth himself shall be abased; and he that humbleth himself shall be exalted." (Luke 18:14 KJV)

Peter wrote about humility, "Humble yourselves therefore under the mighty hand of God, that he may exalt you in due time:" (1 Peter 5:6 KJV) Humility is all throughout the Bible, Jesus was humble and Jesus is our role model. Paul wrote about the humility of Christ in Philippians "and being found in fashion as a man, he humbled himself, and became obedient unto death, even the death of the cross." (Philippians 2:8 KJV)

Very similar to pride is flattery[156]. Looking back over my life, I could have avoid lots of grief if I would have simply avoided people that flattered. "A lying tongue hateth those that are afflicted by it; And a flattering mouth worketh ruin." (Proverbs 26:28) KJV "A man

---

[156] Insincere praise

that flattereth his neighbour Spreadeth a net for his feet." (Proverbs 29:5 KJV)

Love is the Fulfillment of the Law

Jesus said:

> Think not that I am come to destroy the law, or the prophets: I am not come to destroy, but to fulfil.
>
> Matthew 5:17 KJV

What did Jesus mean when he said he came to fulfill the law and the prophets? When the Sadducees and the Pharisees were testing Jesus in the 22nd chapter of Matthew, a Pharisee came up to Jesus and asked Jesus what was the greatest commandment:

> Master, which is the great commandment in the law? Jesus said unto him, Thou shalt love the Lord thy God with all thy heart, and with all thy soul, and with all thy mind. This is the first and great commandment. And the second is like unto it, Thou shalt love thy neighbour as thyself. On these two commandments hang all the law and the prophets.
>
> Matthew 22:36-40 KJV

"On these two commandments hang all the law and the prophets." I believe that Jesus is saying that all of the law and the prophets concern us loving God with all our heart, soul and mind and loving our neighbors as ourselves. Every law and commandment points back to love; love of our God and love of our neighbors. Paul explains that love is the fulfilling of the law in the 13th chapter of Romans:

> Owe no man any thing, but to love one another: for he that loveth another hath fulfilled the law. For this, Thou shalt not commit adultery, Thou shalt not kill, Thou shalt not steal, Thou shalt not bear false witness, Thou shalt not covet; and if there be any other commandment, it is briefly comprehended in this saying, namely, Thou shalt love thy neighbour as thyself. Love worketh no ill to his neighbour: therefore love is the fulfilling of the law.
>
> Romans 13:8-10 KJV

We Must Allow Christ to Change Our Hearts

During the Sermon on the Mount Jesus explain that it is not enough for us to refrain from the physical acts prohibited by the commandments; that we must change our hearts as well:

> Ye have heard that it was said by them of old time, Thou shalt not commit adultery: but I say unto you, That whosoever looketh on a woman to lust after her hath committed adultery with her already in his heart.

Matthew 5:27-28 KJV

We should be pursuing a change of our hearts in order to draw our hearts near Jesus, heart focused, love for Christ, and love for our neighbors. I find it helpful to pray for God to change my heart, to fill my heart with love. When I struggle with judgement of others and struggle to forgive others I pray and ask God to help me to not judge others and to help me to forgive them[157].

It is possible to not commit the act of adultery and not to commit the act of murder, but to still be a lustful and hateful person. Jesus is giving us a higher standard, which requires a change heart.

The Gospel of Christ is heart focused:

> For out of the heart proceed evil thoughts, murders, adulteries, fornications, thefts, false witness, blasphemies: these are the things which defile a man: but to eat with unwashen hands defileth not a man.

Matthew 15:16-20 KJV

Focusing on conforming our physical actions is like treating the symptoms of a sickness. The reason that the Pharisees and Sadducees were such hypocrites is because as humans we can't do what God wants us to do through our own power. If we try to make ourselves in the image of Christ without changing our heart we will be miserable, because we can't do it without the power of the Holy Spirit which helps us to change our hearts.

---

[157] When someone has a "forgiveness" problem, often times it is a repentance problem, because if they were in touch with how broken they were, they would not deny forgiveness to others.

We cannot change without Christ:

> Abide in me, and I in you. As the branch cannot bear fruit of itself, except it abide in the vine; no more can ye, except ye abide in me. I am the vine, ye are the branches: He that abideth in me, and I in him, the same bringeth forth much fruit: for without me ye can do nothing.

John 15:4-5 KJV

We are called to love God and our fellow man, as God loves us and we can only do that through our faith in Christ, which works by love and the power of the Holy Spirit. We should be praying for God to change our hearts, to help us love the Lord our God with all our mind, our heart and our soul and to help us love our neighbors as ourselves. We should be praying not only for our forgiveness, but with the power to forgive others. We should be asking God to remove anything from our hearts and lives that prevents us from drawing closer to Him. As a Christian, our number one goal in this life should be to glorify God and get as close to God as possible, before our physical death. For a Christian, what else is there?

Salvation

The third chapter of John records Jesus's conversation with Nicodemus, reading John 3 we learn about salvation "Jesus answered and said unto him, Verily, verily, I say unto thee, Except a man be born again, he cannot see the kingdom of God." (John 3:3 KJV) Nicodemus questions how a man can be "born again" and Jesus goes on to explain "...Except a man be born of water and of the Spirit, he cannot enter into the kingdom of God. That which is born of the flesh is flesh; and that which is born of the Spirit is spirit." (John 3:5-6 KJV)

Later in that conversation, Jesus speaks the most well known bible verse of all time:

> For God so loved the world, that he gave his only begotten Son, that whosoever believeth in him should not perish, but have everlasting life.

John 3:16 KJV

Jesus is the only mediator between man and God "For there is one God, and one mediator between God and men, the man Christ Jesus;" (1 Timothy 2:5 KJV) Jesus Christ, who was sinless, laid down his life for us "No man taketh it from me, but I lay it down of myself. I have power to lay it down, and I have power to take it again. This commandment have I received of my Father." (John 10:18 KJV) Jesus laid down his life to bring us to God, "For Christ also hath once suffered for sins, the just for the unjust, that he might bring us to God..." (1 Peter 3:18 KJV) Not only did Christ die for us he died for us on the cross while we were sinners, "But God commendeth his love toward us, in that, while we were yet sinners, Christ died for us. Much more then, being now justified by his blood, we shall be saved from wrath through him." (Romans 5:8-9 KJV)

Jesus has done for us what we cannot do on our own, we do not deserve it, we cannot earn it, all we can do is accept Him "Behold, I stand at the door, and knock: if any man hear my voice, and open the door, I will come in to him, and will sup with him, and he with me." (Revelation 3:20 KJV) To accept Christ you must confess with your mouth and believe in your heart that God raised Jesus from the dead, "that if thou shalt confess with thy mouth the Lord Jesus, and shalt believe in thine heart that God hath raised him from the dead, thou shalt be saved. For with the heart man believeth unto righteousness; and with the mouth confession is made unto salvation." (Romans 10:9-10 KJV)

Here's a prayer you can pray to receive Christ:

> Dear God, I know that I am a sinner. I want to turn from my sins, and I ask for Your forgiveness. I believe that Jesus Christ is Your Son. I believe He died for my sins and that You raised Him to life. I want Him to come into my heart and to take control of my life. I want to trust Jesus as my Savior and follow Him as my Lord from this day forward. In Jesus' Name, amen.

Growing in Our Relationship With God

The first thing I would tell anyone that was trying to grow their relationship with God is to read your Bible. You have to read your Bible and you should want to read your Bible, as Christians we are supposed to "...hunger and thirst after righteousness..." (Matthew 5:6 KJV) How are we going to know what righteousness is without reading the Bible?

In his second epistle, the Apostle Peter said, "grace and peace be multiplied unto you through the knowledge of God, and of Jesus our Lord," (2 Peter 1:2 KJV). Grace and peace are multiplied unto us "through the knowledge of God, and Jesus our Lord" and we gain knowledge God through the reading of His Word, the Bible. In the gospel of John, we learn that Jesus is the Word. "In the beginning was the Word, and the Word was with God, and the Word was God." (John 1:1 KJV) "And the Word was made flesh, and dwelt among us, (and we beheld his glory, the glory as of the only begotten of the Father,) full of grace and truth." (John 1:14 KJV)

I do not claim to understand how Jesus is the "Word", the Son of God, and dwelt among us: but there are many things about the Bible that I do not understand. "For my thoughts are not your thoughts, neither are your ways my ways, saith the LORD. For as the heavens are higher than the earth, so are my ways higher than your ways, and my thoughts than your thoughts." (Isaiah 55:8-9 KJV) Just as nobody can fully understand or explain the Trinity, there are many things in the Bible that we can not fully comprehend, things that we must except on faith. But, it is "through the knowledge of God, and Jesus our Lord" that grace and peace is multiplied to us. We are told to, "Study to shew thyself approved unto God, a workman that needeth not to be ashamed, rightly dividing the word of truth." (2 Timothy 2:15 KJV)

Not only are we supposed to read the Bible, we are supposed to "meditate" on the Bible day and night. "Blessed is the man that walketh not in the counsel of the ungodly, nor standeth in the way of sinners, Nor sitteth in the seat of the scornful. But his delight is in the law of the LORD; And in his law doth he meditate day and night." (Psalm 1:1-2 KJV)

Jesus also instructed us in the fifteenth chapter of John that His words should abide in us:

> Now ye are clean through the word which I have spoken unto you. Abide in me, and I in you. As the branch cannot bear fruit of itself, except it abide in the vine; no more can ye, except ye abide in me. I am the vine, ye are the branches: He

that abideth in me, and I in him, the same bringeth forth much fruit: for without me ye can do nothing. If a man abide not in me, he is cast forth as a branch, and is withered; and men gather them, and cast them into the fire, and they are burned. If ye abide in me, and my words abide in you, ye shall ask what ye will, and it shall be done unto you. Herein is my Father glorified, that ye bear much fruit; so shall ye be my disciples.

John 15:3-8 KJV

If I had accepted Christ as my savior and did not have a desire to read, learn, and study His Word; I would be praying about that daily until that desire manifested itself in my life.

I find it helpful to begin each day by reading the chapter of Proverbs that corresponds with the day of the month, this allows me to read the book of Proverbs every month. I also enjoy reading five chapters of Psalms, there are 150 chapters of Pslams and by reading 5 chapters a day you can make it through the entire book of Pslams in a month. (Multiply the day of the month times 5 and that is the point you need to finish for that day.) There is so much packed into Proverbs and Psalms, they are an endless blessing. Proverbs and Pslams are so great because they teach us how this world actually works. "The fear of the LORD is the beginning of knowledge: But fools despise wisdom and instruction." (Proverbs 1:7 KJV) Growing up I was always trying to "figure out" how the world actually worked. Proverbs and Psalms will tell you how the world actually works. "All scripture is given by inspiration of God, and is profitable for doctrine, for reproof, for correction, for instruction in rightcousness:" (2 Timothy 3:16 KJV)

Ecclesiastes also teaches us how the world actually works. It was written by King Solomon almost 3,000 years ago and it is amazing how accurate his description of both human behavior and society is. One of my favorite versus was written by King Solomon:

> If you see the oppression of the poor, and the violent perversion of justice and righteousness in a province, do not marvel at the matter; for high official watches over high official, and higher officials are over them.

Ecclesiastes 5:8 NKJV

In Ecclesiastes King Solomon describes everything he did to "seek and search out by wisdom concerning all that is done under heaven,"[158] and King Solomon gives us his conclusion in the last chapter of Ecclesiastes:

> Let us hear the conclusion of the whole matter: Fear God and keep His commandments, For this is man's all. For God will bring every work into judgment, Including every secret thing, Whether good or evil.

Ecclesiastes 12:13-14 NKJV

I would advise any new Christian to start studying the Gospels; Matthew, Mark, Luke, and John. I would read and re-read the Gospels until I knew them. Then once I had a solid foundation in the Gospels I would start reading the rest of the New Testament. I find it helpful to read the scriptures out loud, I want to see, speak it and hear it. And when I find my mind wondering, I start over and re-read what I was not focused on. You have to make yourself focus on the Word of God. You have to know the Word of God, otherwise people can tell you anything.

In addition to studying the Bible, you have to pray. The Apostle Paul said "Pray without ceasing." (1 Thessalonians 5:17 KJV) Jesus went away frequently to pray privately, "And when he had sent them away, he departed into a mountain to pray." (Mark 6:46 KJV) Prayer should not be something you just do with other Christians, "But thou, when thou prayest, enter into thy closet, and when thou hast shut thy door, pray to thy Father which is in secret; and thy Father which seeth in secret shall reward thee openly." (Matthew 6:6 KJV)

Prayer also keeps us from entering into temptation "Watch and pray, that ye enter not into temptation: the spirit indeed is willing, but the flesh is weak." (Matthew 26:41 KJV)

Not only are we supposed to pray for those we love and care about we are supposed to "...pray for them which despitefully use you." (Luke 6:28 KJV) I heard Billy Graham say in an interview one time that one of his biggest regrets is that he had not prayed enough,

---

[158] Ecclesiastes 1:12-13 NKJV

if Billy Graham felt he had not prayed enough, I know that I am really behind.

We also have to praise[159] God, both in our thankfulness and in praise and worship. "Because thy lovingkindness Is better than life, My lips shall praise thee." (Psalm 63:3 KJV); "By him therefore let us offer the sacrifice of praise to God continually, that is, the fruit of our lips giving thanks to his name." (Hebrews 13:15 KJV); "I will praise thee, O LORD, with my whole heart; I will shew forth all thy marvellous works." (Psalm 9:1 KJV); "Is any among you afflicted? let him pray. Is any merry? let him sing psalms." (James 5:13 KJV); "speaking to yourselves in psalms and hymns and spiritual songs, singing and making melody in your heart to the Lord;" (Ephesians 5:19 KJV); and "I will worship toward thy holy temple, and praise thy name for thy lovingkindness and for thy truth: For thou hast magnified thy word above all thy name." (Psalm 138:2 KJV)

True Peace Can Only be Found in Christ

True peace, can only be found in Christ, "And the peace of God, which passeth all understanding, shall keep your hearts and minds through Christ Jesus." (Philippians 4:7 KJV) See also; "Peace I leave with you, my peace I give unto you: not as the world giveth, give I unto you. Let not your heart be troubled, neither let it be afraid." (John 14:27 KJV)

---

[159] You may want to read Acts 16:16-34, where Paul and Silas were praising God while in prison.

www.ingramcontent.com/pod-product-compliance
Lightning Source LLC
Chambersburg PA
CBHW070143230526
45471CB00002B/489